RUGBY

Colin Herridge
Derek Wyatt

2011

THE TEAMS • THE STARS
THE HISTORY OF THE WORLD CUP

endeavour

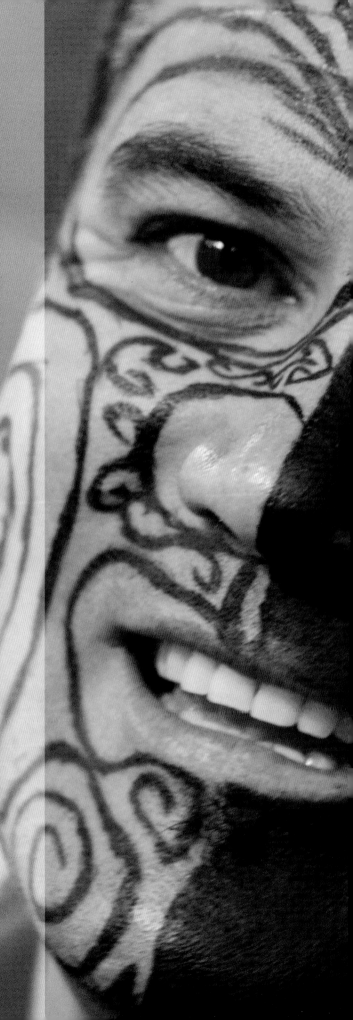

ACKNOWLEDGEMENTS

Endeavour London Ltd.
21-31 Woodfield Road,
London W9 2BA
Fax 44 (0) 20 3227 2432
info@endeavourlondon.com

ISBN: 978-1-908271-08-2

Printed in Italy

Project Manager & Research: Benjamin Bonarius
Designer: Ros Holder
Production Manager: Mary Osborne

All images courtesy of Getty Images including the
following which have additional attributions:

Agence France Presse: 2, 11br, 12b, 13b, 14b, 18,
22, 24l, 24r, 27, 28, 34tl, 34tm, 35tr, 37tl, 37tr, 37b,
39t, 40r, 41t, 41m, 43tr, 44r, 46, 47t, 53m, 53b, 56,
59t, 59b, 60, 61br, 62br, 63t, 63b, 68l, 68r, 69tr,
69br, 69bl, 71t, 73m, 73b, 74t, 74b, 75, 78l, 78r,
79m, 79b, 81bl, 83bl, 90, 91b, 93t, 95t, 95ml, 95mr,
95b, 98b, 99t, 99m, 99b, 100t, 104, 108l, 108r, 111t;
Bob Thomas: 6t, 6b, 7t, 7mr, 7ml, 7bl, 8tl, 8ml, 9br;
Gallo Images: 10mr, 18, 80l, 80r, 83tl, 84t, 85t, 85b;
LatinContent: 47m, 47b, 48tl, 48tr, 48b, 49t.

Previous page: The All Blacks perform the Haka,
before a match against South Africa in Richmond,
Surrey, 1916.

Right: Vivid and vibrant New Zealander supporter, at
the World Cup quarter-final match against France in
Cardiff, 6 October, 2007.

CONTENTS

NAU MAI
A NOTE FROM THE AUTHORS

The largest, longest and loudest ever rugby party in the world will begin on 9 September, 2011 in the North and South Islands of the great country of New Zealand, famous for many things, not least of which is its rugby. The All Black nation promises not just amazing sport for the seventh Rugby World Cup, but has taken to its heart a desire to show the world it has more to offer us than just an oval ball, the more poignant after the two earthquakes in September, 2010 and February, 2011 in Christchurch. The earthquakes caused tragic loss of life and property, including Lancaster Park, but the true grit of New Zealand has shown through.

For just over six weeks, visitors to the Islands will experience a heady cocktail of stunning scenery mixing mountains and beaches, some of the best wines in the world – worth putting down in more ways than one – a galaxy of great restaurants and pubs, all backed up by its own melee of wonderful people whose influence in the world goes way beyond its shores.

New Zealanders have a proud sporting tradition, not least as hosts going back to the Commonwealth Games in Auckland in 1990, the Cricket World Cup in 1992, the America's Cup 2003 and the British and Irish Lions tour to New Zealand 2005, but all of these pale before the scale of the Rugby World Cup.

The All Blacks do not need reminding that they haven't won the Rugby World Cup since they co-hosted the inaugural event back in 1987. They are the "nearly" men of Rugby World Cups. Over seven World Cups, New Zealand has won one title and lost another whilst Australia won two and lost one and South Africa has already won two, even though they were only admitted in 1995. England has made it to the final three times and came away the winner once. Back in 1987, scrum halves put the ball in straight to the scrums; there was no lifting in the line-outs; there were rucks with scars to show for it. In 1987 the game was still largely amateur and South Africa had yet to experience the Mandela magic. It seemed a long time ago. It was.

Above: Crusaders players observe a minute of silence for victims of the Pike River mine disaster and the Christchurch earthquake during the round three Super Rugby match between the Crusaders and the Waratahs at Trafalgar Park on 4 March, 2011 in Nelson, New Zealand.

Colin Herridge
Derek Wyatt

1987 TO 2003

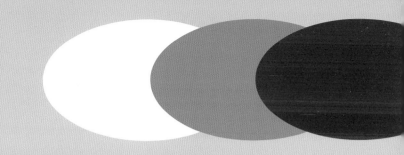

The British and Irish Lions

Prior to the World Cup, international competitions were largely limited to the four Home Unions (England, Ireland, Scotland and Wales) and British and Irish Lions tours. The Lions tours had a long history. Tours to New Zealand took place in 1888 and to South Africa in 1910. They were much looked forward to by the players, but the results made for uncomfortable reading. It wasn't until 1971 that the Lions beat the All Blacks and 1974 that they defeated the Springboks.

Birth of the World Cup

It was no surprise to find that there was little glee amongst the blazers of the Four Nations at the idea of a Rugby World Cup. The die-hards were worried that the game could go professional, more so following the Adidas boot money scandal which broke in 1982 where a number of Four Nations players had accepted small amounts of cash (between £50 and £200) to wear Adidas rugby boots. Though there was a lot of huffing and puffing, not a single player was suspended.

When the IRB finally accepted a joint Australian and New Zealand proposal in 1985 for a one-off Rugby World Cup in 1987 the die was cast. The problem was that not one of the Four Nations was ready for such a tournament. Indeed, surveying the World Cup results since then, only England has had any kind of success though France has been more consistent, qualifying for five out of six semi-finals.

Left: Fergus Slattery of the British Lions with Willie John McBride's pipe during the Lions tour of South Africa, 1974.
Below: Mervyn Davies of the British Lions runs with the ball during the their tour match against South Africa in 1974.

The First World Cup

The cat was out of the bag and what had been intended as a one-off World Cup in 1987 quickly transformed itself into a regular four-year affair. In 1986, the IOC decided to separate out its Summer and Winter Games and by 1994 the Winter Games began a four-year cycle with the Summer Games every leap year (1992, 1996…). The result was that the Winter Games vied for sports marketing budgets against the FIFA World Cup (1994, 1998…). Rugby's masters intended that the RWC would find its own niche without having to worry too much about rival sporting championships, save perhaps for the IAAF Track & Field World Championships.

Left: Mike Harrison of England powers through the Japan defence during the World Cup match in Sydney, Australia, 30 May, 1987. England won 60-7.

Above: Scotland celebrate beating France to win the Grand Slam at Murrayfield, 17 September, 1984. Left to Right: Colin Deans, Jim Calder, Roger Baird and Roy Laidlaw. Not long after this the IRB accepted the proposal for a Rugby World Cup.

Right: Brian Spillane of Ireland in action against Wales during the World Cup match held in Wellington on 25 May, 1987. Wales won 13-6.

Below: In the early 1980s Rugby Union was still very much an amateur sport. Welsh international Bleddyn Bowen on duty at Port Talbot Police Station, 1984.

Left: Steve Sutton and Richard Moriarty of Wales jumping against Gary Whetton of New Zealand during the semi-final at the 1987 World Cup in Brisbane, 14 June. Wales were the only Home Nations team to reach the semi-finals. They lost to New Zealand 49-6.

Top: Matt Duncan of Scotland in action against Zimbabwe during a World Cup match in Wellington, New Zealand, 30 May, 1987. Scotland beat Zimbabwe 60-21.

Above: Robert Jones of Wales is seen in action against England in the quarter-final in Brisbane, 8 June, 1987. Wales won 16-3.

1991 World Cup

Of course, it was no real surprise that the final of the Rugby World Cup for 1991 should come "home" to Twickenham. Unfortunately, its organisation left a lot to be desired. The players were waking up to the fact the game was going global while the game's administrators were still lost in some kind of post-colonial haze. Crowds flocked to watch the games; ITV outbid the BBC for the television coverage – a first – and immediately asked the IRB to change "half-time" as they needed to broadcast their advertisements. Another first was achieved as players came off the pitch for five minutes and the era of the professional coaching staff began. Previously only the captain could say anything at half time, now the coach began to supersede the captain in importance.

In the final preparation before the World Cup, England made their base at Tylney Hall, a country hotel, near Basingstoke. There was still an air of " ' 'lads on tour' which was an integral part of the amateur ethos; the players had little understanding of nutrition and how to peak, physically and mentally. The old-fashioned rugby drinking culture was evident during a two-day break to Jersey, with wives and girlfriends, in the midst of the pool games.

In the quarter-final between Ireland and Australia played in Dublin, Gordon Hamilton, the Irish flanker, outpaced man-of-the-match David Campese to score. A conversion gave the home side the lead by 18-15, but as the clock ticked for full-time, Campese passed the ball to Michael Lynagh who scored a try for victory.

In the final at Twickenham, in front of a partisan crowd, England knew it was their time. They tried to beat Australia by playing a more expansive game than they had done previously when they had trundled forward to put Rob

Top: Mike Teague of England (centre) holds onto the ball with the help of Brian Moore (left) in the match against Italy during the 1991 World Cup at Twickenham, England. England won the game 36-6.
Middle: England's Rob Andrew kicks a drop goal as Scottish players attempt a charge down. England won 9-6 at Murrayfield, 26 October, 1991.
Left: A rear view of a collapsed scrum during the World Cup match between Scotland and Ireland at Murrayfield in Edinburgh, Scotland, 12 October, 1991. Scotland won the match 24-15.

Andrew in kicking range. This did not work and Australia won by 12-6, becoming the second winners of the William Webb Ellis Trophy. The feeling in the England camp was summed up by the England hooker, Brian Moore, "In 1991 it was our event, our crowds, our fervour, our home. Everything was in our hands and we had blown the tactics in the final. We were superior in the final and did not cash in on it."

At the end of the day, the most significant point about the 1991 World Cup was that two sides outside the top eight nations (Western Samoa and Canada) reached the quarter-finals and acquitted themselves well. It was hoped that this was a prelude to what might happen in future tournaments, but as will be seen, only Argentina has so far really challenged the status quo.

Top Left: Phil May of Wales with his arm in a sling looks dejected on the bench in the Wales v Western Samoa match during the 1991 World Cup at Cardiff Arms Park in Cardiff, Wales. Western Samoa won the match 16-13.

Middle Left: Gordon Hamilton of Ireland is mobbed after scoring the near-winner against Australia in the quarter-final of the Rugby World Cup match played at Lansdowne Road, Dublin.

Bottom Left: Simon Poidevin, Phil Kearns, and Michael Lynagh of Australia hold the Webb Ellis Trophy in the baths after the 1991 World Cup final. Australia beat England 12 points to 6 in the final at Twickenham.

Below: Frank Bunce of Western Samoa (with the ball) outjumps Wales fullback Michael Rayer during the World Cup match in Cardiff on 6 October, 1991. Western Samoa won 16-13.

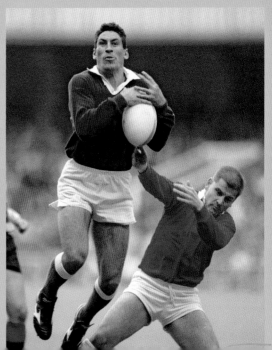

1995 World Cup

The World Cup was the first major sporting event to take place in South Africa following the end of apartheid. It was also the last major event of Rugby Union's amateur era; two months after the tournament, the IRFB opened the sport to professionalism. After an IRB meeting in Paris in August 1995, without any formal vote of the board, Chairman Vernon Pugh simply announced that the game had gone professional.

Nelson Mandela and Francois Pienaar's roles in the World Cup later became the subject of a film and a television documentary. It was an extraordinary event, made notable by South Africa's victory on home soil.

Top left: Will Carling (left) with Dewi Morris of England during training for their opening match against Argentina, 22 May, 1995.

Top Right: England wing Rory Underwood in his full flying gear.

Left: David Campese of Australia is closed down by England's Jeremy Guscott during the 1995 Rugby World Cup match between Australia and England played in Cape Town. England won the match 25-22, November 1995.

Above: South African President Nelson Mandela, dressed in a number 6 Springbok jersey, congratulates Springbok Captain Francois Pienaar after their victory over the All Blacks 15-12 in the final, 24 June, 1995.

Top left: Mike Hall of Wales uses his pace to charge through during the 1995 Rugby World Cup Pool C match between Japan and Wales held on 27 May, 1995 at the Free State Stadium, in Bloemfontein. Wales won the match 57-10.

Middle left: Sean Fitzpatrick of New Zealand on the charge during the Rugby World Cup match against Scotland played in Pretoria, South Africa. New Zealand won the match 48-30.

Bottom left: Jonah Lomu of New Zealand breaks free of the Welsh defence during the 1995 Rugby World Cup Pool C match between New Zealand and Wales held on 31 May, 1995 at Ellis Park, in Johannesburg. New Zealand won the match 34-9.

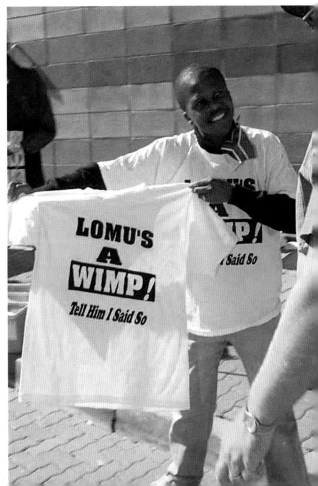

Below: A vendor sells a disparaging T-shirt outside Johannesburg's Ellis Park before the Rugby World Cup final on 24 June, 1995.

1999 World Cup

In the four years after the Springboks had won the Cup, the game changed beyond recognition. The RWC 1999 was moved back again to the UK and France. It was the first in the new professional era with Wales as the main host. It had been touch-and-go whether the Millennium Stadium in Cardiff (replacing the Arms Park) would actually be ready in time for the opening ceremony and game. It was. Just.

A new Tri Nations Cup and a Super 12 Club involving South Africa, New Zealand and Australia on a home and away basis drew huge crowds. Rugby beat to a faster tune in the Southern Hemisphere and it was no surprise that all three reached the semi-finals in 1999.

RWC 99 saw some unfortunate mismatches. In the pools there were 17 matches where the winning side scored more than 40 points; several matches had margins of about 100 points.

By common consent, England had a pretty awful tournament. It was, however, a propitious first for Clive Woodward as coach and the boyish, modest 20-year-old, Jonny Wilkinson. Wilkinson notched up a cool 20 points in the thrashing of Italy 67-7. Such was his unerring success that his hallmark, slow, slightly stuttering left foot conversions, were soon being copied throughout the land. By the end of the 2007 tournament he had topped the most-points scored with 249 points.

France caused the upset of the tournament by beating favourites New Zealand in a semi-final, but they ran out of gas in the World Cup final and lost 35-12 to the likeable Australians.

Opposite above left and right: Keith Wood is tackled in Ireland's unsuccessful match against Australia and fisticuffs break out in the same match, which resulted in Toutai Kefu being banned for two weeks whilst Ireland's Trevor Brennan was suspended for 10 days.
Opposite middle: The scoreboard says it all, a bad mismatch.
Opposite bottom: Welsh fans celebrating the opening ceremony, 1 October, 1999.
Above left and right: England coach Clive Woodward celebrates defeating Tonga and Jonny Wilkinson kicks.
Right: Welsh fullback Shane Howarth flanked by his teammates at the end of the quarter-final with Australia, which they lost 24-9, at the Millennium Stadium in Cardiff, 23 October, 1999.

2003 World Cup

The 2003 World Cup is remembered for Jonny Wilkinson and that famous dropped goal. England versus Australia was the final most neutral supporters wanted to see. England had entered the contest as joint favourites. Australia were the hosts and, of course, it was the Northern Hemisphere against the Southern Hemisphere. To win, England would have to defeat the most competitive rugby nation in the world, already with two World Cups under her belt.

Top left: During their 2003 summer tour, England scored a rare victory (15-13) over New Zealand. Here captain Martin Johnson shakes the hand of Ma'a Nonu, at Westpac Stadium, Wellington.

Top right: The England and Wales forwards clash in the scrum during the quarter-final match at Suncorp Stadium, 9 November, 2003, in Brisbane.

Above: Kiwi-born French player Tony Marsh is dragged down in a tackle by Brian O'Driscoll, during the France v Ireland quarter-final match which France won 43-21 at the Telstradome, Melbourne, 9 November, 2003.

Left: Scottish lock Stuart Grimes is lifted by teammates during their quarter-final match against Australia at the Suncorp Stadium in Brisbane, 8 November, 2003. Australia defeated Scotland 33-16.

On the big day warm rain fell. It worsened by kick-off. Surprisingly, the Wallabies struck first and early with a cross kick from Stephen Larkham which saw Lote Tuqiri easily out-jump the small, but perfectly formed, Jason Robinson to score. Yet, by half time the twinkle-toed Robinson had scored his own try, following three penalties from Jonny Wilkinson to give England a 14-5 lead at half time. It ought to have been more, as Ben Kay somehow lost the ball on the line. England's forwards had total dominance in the line-out and it was hard to know how Australia would find a way back into the game. Could England really win their first World Cup?

Right: Lote Tuqiri and Jason Robinson jump for the ball during the final in Sydney, 22 November, 2003.
Bottom left and right: England team huddle before the semi-final match with France; Ben Cohen of England hands off Aurelien Rougerie at Telstra Stadium 16 November, 2003 in Sydney. England won 24-7.

Yet, England failed to ram home their advantage and worse, failed to add to their score. Australia subbed their second rows and gradually edged level with three penalty goals by Flately to take the game into extra time.

Jonny Wilkinson scored a penalty, Flately replied... and then having tried and failed three times, England's talisman finally dropped that famous goal, albeit with his right foot, to win the Cup 20-17. The din from English supporters was overwhelming.

That day, 22 November 2003, is a day that remains imprinted on many a rugby fan and for at least one lucky witness, and author, an abiding memory was of Martin Johnson, heroic Captain, walking quietly, a couple of miles, and then some, to his hotel in the pouring rain at five in the morning. A great victory.

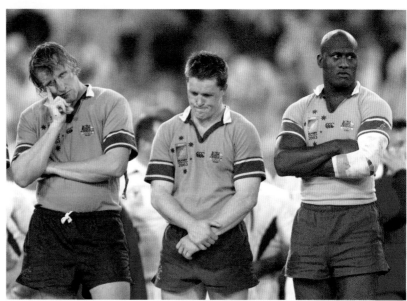

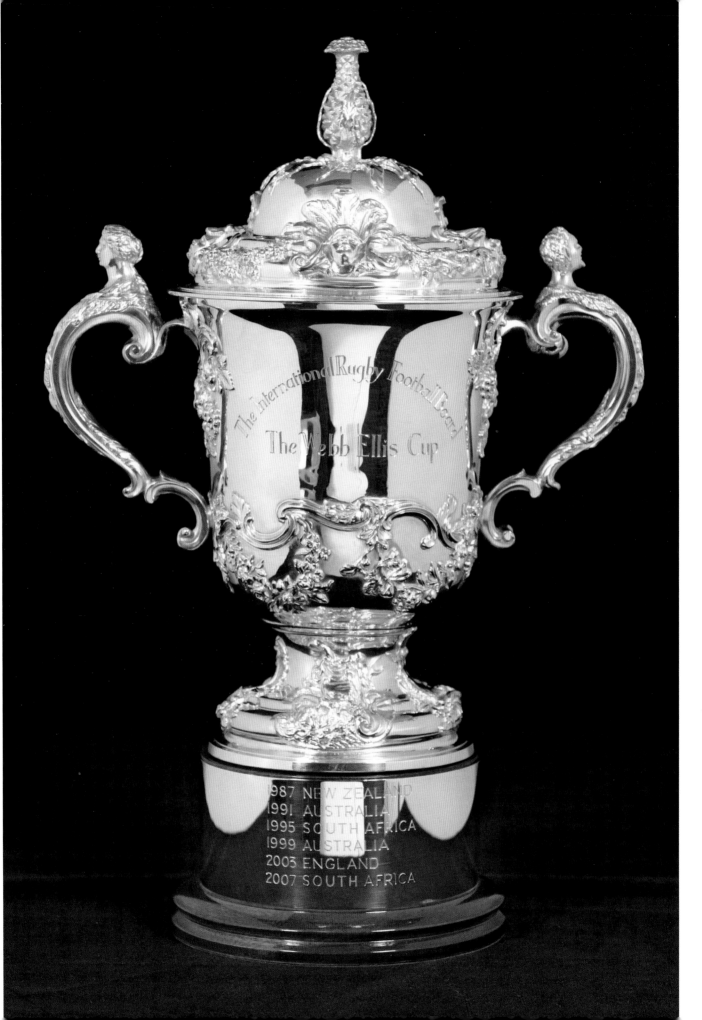

The International Rugby Football Board

The Webb Ellis Cup

1987 NEW ZEALAND
1991 AUSTRALIA
1995 SOUTH AFRICA
1999 AUSTRALIA
2003 ENGLAND
2007 SOUTH AFRICA

2007 to 2011

Rugby World Cup 2007 Reprise

Argentina breaks through; NZ loses again to the French; SA crowned Champions

In order to win the bid for Rugby World Cup 2007, the French Federation had to seek support from their counterparts in Wales and Scotland, which meant they had to relocate four matches to Cardiff and two to Edinburgh. This happened despite the International Rugby Board's (IRB) own recommendations following the unsatisfactory RWC 1991 – when the competition was held in five countries with four legal systems using three currencies – that it should go to a single country. England were the under-bidders for 2007; they had unsuccessfully proposed a senior and junior Rugby World Cup which seemed too much of a change for dyed-in-the-wool executive members of the IRB.

In the past the Rugby World Cup has sometimes been shared by more than one country, but was an outstanding success when run by a single country, as in South Africa in 1995 and Australia in 2003. It is good news that RWC looks set to emulate this with New Zealand for 2011, England for 2015 and Japan for 2019. The IRB seems to have finally taken its own advice.

placement of upcoming World Cup venues will depend to a degree on the result of RWC 2011. If a Samoa, a Fiji or a Tonga ends up with Argentina in the semi-finals, for instance, who knows where popular support and enthusiasm will entice the RWC to travel to next. However, semi-final results of this sort are unlikely, despite Fiji's valiant 16-16 draw against Wales last November at the Millennium Stadium.

We must also not forget Argentina's heroic victory over France in the opening of the tournament which may presage a very exciting future. Sometimes, results like these can flatter to deceive, but the Pumas – playing in the so-called pool of death which also included Ireland – topped their group. They then went on to beat Scotland 19-13 in the quarter-finals (Argentina was previously a quarter-finalist in 1999) to reach the semi-finals for the first time, but lost to South Africa 37-13 in a brutal match. It was a game too far for them but it was a resounding success for this football-mad nation, especially

Looking back, RWC 2007 may now be viewed as the watershed World Cup for the *ancien regime* of England, Wales, Scotland, Ireland, France, South Africa, New Zealand and Australia who have dominated when the World Cup is played. The

Previous page: Captain John Smit holding up the William Webb Ellis Trophy after South Africa beat England in the final of the 2007 World Cup in Paris. Also in the picture is South African President at the time, Thabo Mbeki.
Below: Fijian winger, Michael Tagicakibau, having his shirt pulled in vain by Welsh forward, Dan Lydiate, in the match at Cardiff in November 2010, which was drawn 16 points all.
Right: Australian full back, Kurtley Beale, on the attack during a Tri Nations game between South Africa and Australia in Bloemfontein, South Africa, September 2010.

as at that time they did not have a domestic professional Rugby Union structure and they had to rely heavily on overseas Argentine players, diligently working in Italy, France, England and Ireland. Notwithstanding, in the absurd non-match, the third place play-off, which the IRB insists on, Argentina again beat France 34-10.

It has taken Argentina four years of lobbying and harrying the IRB and SANZAR (the Tri Nations organisers) for them to be included in the Southern Hemisphere's competition. Now that they are there, it is important for the development of the game in the Americas that Argentina's results in 2007 are repeated in 2011 before the Tri Nations becomes the Four Nations in 2012.

Argentina's shock result against France in the opener wasn't the only surprise in what developed into the best-organised World Cup in the Northern Hemisphere. South Africa announced her arrival by thrashing a woeful England in her second game by 36-0, prompting calls from many quarters, including RFU Committee grandees, that Brian Ashton, the England coach, and his back-room staff should be fired immediately. Fortunately, they felt a little differently in the morning.

It is a truism that the All Blacks usually spend their time between World Cups thrashing teams, whether home or away. Between the two Rugby World Cups of 2003 and 2007 they remained undefeated against all of the Six Nation sides home and away. Only South Africa and occasionally Australia offered any resistance. And as they had done in 1991, 1995 and 1999, they arrived at the World Cup as the favourites. And as they had done previously, they topped their group with some outstanding displays. And as they had done previously, they failed to deliver once they had gone beyond the first stage of a World Cup.

In 1991, the All Blacks lost in the semi-finals to Australia by 16-6. They were outplayed, with Australia beating them in the tight and completely wrapping up the All Black midfield. The game turned on two marvellous pieces of improvisation and brilliance by David Campese. First he stood at outside half, took the ball from a pass by Nick Farr-Jones and ran on a long arc from right to left. No All Black committed to tackling him and by the time they saw the

danger it was too late. Campese scored in the left hand corner. Then Michael Lynagh chipped the ball over the New Zealand defence, Campese gathered and, as he was about to be submerged by covering tacklers, he flipped the ball over his shoulder to Tim Horan who was coming up fast in support. Without Campese ever seeing him, Horan took the ball in his stride and scored for Lynagh to convert. The score was then 13-0 and the All Blacks had to spend the rest of the game in 'catch up' mode. Grant Fox kicked two penalties but it was not nearly enough and Australia won 16 points to 6.

But it was their capitulation in another semi-final eight years later which stunned the rugby world. In 1999, in the semi-final at Twickenham against France, the All Blacks were 24-10 ahead after only 35 minutes and seemingly already had one hand on the Cup. There was then one of those sublime sweeping movements from under their own posts which saw the French score at the other end and change the nature of the game. The smallest man on the field, Christophe Dominici, got into his stride with a number of mazy runs and the New Zealanders were unable to cope.

Below: French forward, Abdel Benazzi, charging through against New Zealand, handing off Jeff Wilson in the semi-final of the 1999 World Cup, at Twickenham.

The French confidence visibly erupted with the team following the little maestro's lead. The score was transformed from 10-24 to 43-24 for France. The New Zealand players were reduced to jelly and the French players left the field to a standing ovation which could have been heard in Paris.

The All Blacks conceded 33 points without reply. They had never had 43 points scored against them in a Test. It was all too hard for their coach, John Hart, to bear and he resigned, leaving commentators to add that this defeat was one of the reasons why the ruling New Zealand Government lost the General Election that followed the World Cup.

In 2007 they met France again, though this time in the quarter-final in Cardiff: no-one gave France a hope. The All Blacks were down to 14 men when Damien Traille fed the fly half Frederic Michalak, whose burst of speed took him away from the chasing New Zealand players before he off-loaded to Yannick Jauzion to touch down. Jean-Baptiste Elissalde's conversion put France on top. This single event, albeit with a hint of a forward pass, unhinged the All Blacks; all those pre-tournament wins counted for nothing and once again they succumbed to the big match atmosphere and lost 20-18.

Below: Yannick Jauzion being congratulated by Imanol Harinordoquy, after scoring against New Zealand in the quarter-final of the 2007 World Cup. New Zealand full back Mils Muliaina looks on in despair.
Below Right: Jason Robinson beats Jean-Baptiste Elissalde during the semi-final of the 2007 World Cup between England and France in Paris.

New Zealand had once again failed to take the trophy they thought was theirs. Indeed, apart from the opening Rugby World Cup in 1987 in New Zealand, the All Blacks have only played in one other final. That was in 1995 when many of their players strangely developed food poisoning; this was considered deliberate by many. A curious incident, subsequently lost in all the hoo-ha around South Africa's win later, which was captured brilliantly in John Carlin's book *Playing the Enemy: Nelson Mandela and the Game that*

Made a Nation (2008) and his recent documentary *The 16th Man* (2010), if not quite so convincingly in Clint Eastwood's Tinseltown production of it entitled *Invictus* (2009), starring Morgan Freeman and Matt Damon.

There is only one conclusion for many for all of this: the All Blacks are again favourites for the Rugby World Cup this year and not least because the World Cup will take place in New Zealand where rugby success is at the very core of being a New Zealander. If New Zealand were to lose, the tears of disappointment would certainly lead to severe flooding in both North and South Islands.

We were spoilt watching RWC 2007 unfold. As if it wasn't enough to see Argentina do well and New Zealand beaten against all odds, England suddenly found their form. Or perhaps form might be too strong a word. England surely found their forwards who played out of their skins, taking on what proved to be a somewhat flakier Australian pack in the quarter-finals in Marseilles, just edging it 12-10 to go through to a semi-final against a resurgent France. Suddenly and surprisingly, in what was easily the most unpredictable of World Cups, the four semi-final sides were South Africa (now the favourites) v Argentina and France v England (the outsiders). To the punter, the final everyone wanted was South Africa (Southern Hemisphere) v France (Northern Hemisphere) – especially as France were the hosts.

Indeed, examining the five finals before 2007, all of them had involved a host country making it

Year	Hosts	Final	Winners
1987	NZ	NZ v France	New Zealand
1991	5 nations	Aus v Eng	Australia
1995	South Africa	SA v NZ	South Africa
1999	5 nations	Aus v France	Australia
2003	Australia	Eng v Aus	England
2007	France	SA v Eng	South Africa
And a punt on 2011			
2011	NZ	NZ v SA	South Africa

through (though "5 Nations" in 1991 and 1999 was stretching the analogy a touch) and four of them had been between Northern and Southern Hemisphere countries. So, of course, 2007 was always going to be between South Africa (though rugby romantics would have prayed for Argentina) and France (why spoil the hosting record?).

It took England to upset the *entente cordiale*. Who would have thought this possible after their dreadful opener against South Africa? But against France at Stade Français, as they had done in their previous game against Australia, England's forwards persevered and the French game wilted to a 14-9 loss. Indeed, in some ways the French were beginning to look as though they were the side that always flatters to deceive, always the bridesmaid never the bride, as they have lost both of their two finals (1987 and 1999) and have now lost three semi-finals (1995, 2003 & 2007). Steely-eyed observers might note that their record against England is not good, as they have lost all their games to them – in the quarter-finals in 1991 and the semi-finals in 2003 and now 2007! Can France get the (English) monkey off their back by winning the Rugby World Cup in New Zealand?

In the final, South Africa easily won the line-outs, had a stronger pack and deservedly beat England 15-6 to become the world champions for the second time, thus equalling Australia's record (1991 & 1999). England (as they had done in 1991 against Australia at Twickenham) failed to have a Plan B and yet in both their finals they had opportunities to win their games.

RWC 2007 Conclusions

Despite the fact that games had to be played outside France, RWC 2007 was a stunning success story. The French Federation took the game all over France for the first time and they were rewarded with record crowds and receipts.

Of course, it will always be known as Argentina's break-through into the top echelons of World Cup. Interestingly, none of the second-tier countries have made it past the quarter-finals, and those that have failed to progress through the qualifying rounds at the following World Cup.

A mistake, repeated in RWC 2011, was allowing 20 teams to qualify rather than 16. Actually, a bigger mistake was in not creating a senior and a junior World Cup competition, as proposed by England in her bid. It is of no benefit to any new rugby-playing country to qualify for a World Cup and then be beaten by over 60 points.

Below: Argentina's legendary scrum half, Agustin Pichot clears the ball from the scrum in a quarter-final match against Scotland in October 2007 at Stade de France, Paris.

If 2007 was Argentina's break-through World Cup, 2011 could see a number of countries bidding to do something similar. Whilst all eyes will be on the new boys from Russia making their debut, look out for Fiji, Samoa and Tonga too.

RWC 2011 saw the following countries automatically qualify:

Pool A New Zealand, France & Tonga

Pool B Argentina, England and Scotland

Pool C Australia, Ireland and Italy

Pool D South Africa, Wales and Fiji

This left eight places to play for from Europe, the Americas, the Middle & Far East, Polynesia and Africa. The five champions from each territory qualified and then there were play-offs for the remaining three places.

Russia (known as the Bears) had a tough route to the finals, having to win through the European Nations Cup for Level 2 countries. In the end, by drawing 21-all with Romania in February 2010, they were placed second and guaranteed an automatic World Cup qualification (top two qualify). They then subsequently played Georgia, the top team, in Turkey early in 2011 to determine which team went into Pool B and which into Pool C. Georgia took that match quite easily 36-8, having defeated Spain 17-9 to top the European Nations Cup.

Romania then made it three from Europe when they beat Uruguay in the last of the play-off matches. In Montevideo the scores were level 21-21, but later in Bucharest, Romania claimed the final spot by winning 39-12. Csaba Gal, Alexandru Manta, Catalin Fercu and Madalin Lemnaru all scored tries, and there was also a penalty try. Fly half Danut Dumbrava added 12 points with the boot. Uruguay scored tries through Martin Crosa and Ivo Dugonjic. Before then Romania had had to defeat the African runners-up, Tunisia, 56-13 whilst Uruguay had beaten Kazakhstan 44-7.

Before the break-up of the Soviet Union in 1991, Russia played in an Eastern European Cup alongside Czechoslovakia, Romania (then pushing for entry into the Five Nations) and Poland. England was invited to participate in the Cup in 1977 in Tbilisi, Georgia (then still inside the Soviet tent) but turned it down and sent instead the Penguins RFC who beat the Soviet Union in the final. Rugby in both Russia and Romania has taken a generation to re-group, but they have outstanding athletes in many Olympic sports and with Rugby Sevens being included in the Rio 2016 Olympic Games, it won't be too long before they start to move up the rankings. They may find though that New Zealand is a more hostile environment for them, although their ever-thoughtful management arranged for them to visit New Zealand in January 2011 when they played and beat a Taranaki International XV (33-24) and South Canterbury (31-7).

Below: Romania's Mihai Lazar tries to break through the tackle of Matthias Braun of Uruguay during the World Cup qualifier second-leg match in Bucharest, November 2010. Romania won 61-33.

Below right: Georgia's Malkhaz Urdzhikashvili hands off Spain's Matthew Cook during a World Cup qualifying game in Tblisi, February 2010.

Otherwise there were no real shocks in those countries qualifying for this year's Rugby World Cup. How different it might have been if England had hosted RWC 2007 and the IRB had consented to a Junior World Cup which would have given a real spur to the growth of rugby in Tier 2 and Tier 3 countries.

One of the qualifiers was Canada – ever present since 1987; they again defeated USA, though they lost their first game 12-6 in Charleston before winning 41-18 in Edmonton. This left the USA in a play-off against Uruguay which was much more of a struggle than the score lines suggested, winning (away) 27-22 and 27-6 (home). Poor Uruguay – they deserve a medal of their own for their travails – having to play three sets of play-offs and then fall at the last hurdle to Romania. Canada and The Eagles joined Argentina from the Americas.

past 50 years and continues to this day. Nonetheless, the Sevens successes of Fiji has given rugby a new focus and impetus in the Islands. Their weakness has been a tendency to lose critical matches because of a lack of fitness in the last quarter and by giving silly penalties away. No team will relish their group matches against them. Samoa qualified for New Zealand by beating Papua New Guinea 115-7 and 72-13.

Finally, in Africa Namibia again came through defeating Tunisia, just winning 18-13 in Tunis and more easily 22-10 in Windhoek. Namibia ought really to have made a breakthrough in world rugby by now, but has flattered to deceive.

Below left: Ryan Nicholas of Japan playing in the Asian Five Nations match against Kazakhstan in Tokyo, Japan, May 2010.

Below right: The Namibia players sing their National Anthem prior to their World Cup match against Argentina in September 2007 at the Stade Velodrome, Marseilles, France.

In the Far East, Japan, coached by All Black John Kirwan (a Cup winner in 1987) also qualified for their seventh consecutive World Cup with big wins against Korea (71-13), Hong Kong (94-5), Arabian Gulf and Kazakhstan. Rugby is popular in Japan (as visitors will see when they host RWC 2019), but as fast as they improve they find those countries ahead of them improving too. It's a tough call for them but they have been innovative in the line-outs and loose play and deserve to succeed, and to do so they will have to out-muscle Tonga, New Zealand, France and Canada.

Many followers of the game are confused by the number of Polynesians who move to New Zealand and then qualify for the All Blacks under IRB residency laws. This has denuded their teams – Samoa, Tonga and Fiji – of key players over the

It has been shown in the past that the sides having momentum of successful results going into the World Cups have a much better chance of progressing into the quarter-finals and beyond.

Since the 2007 World Cup the most successful side has been New Zealand. They won the Tri Nations in 2008 and 2010 and had an unbeaten run of 15 games from September 2009 to September 2010 until they lost to Australia in Hong Kong en route to the Northern Hemisphere in November 2010 for their tour, where they went through unbeaten.

South Africa won the Tri Nations in 2009, winning 5 out of the 6 games, but struggled in 2010, although they had a better time than Australia who won only one game in the 2009 competition and did not do much better in 2010.

Above: Welsh captain, Ryan Jones, celebrates with team colleagues after winning the Grand Slam in the Six Nations Championship at the Millennium Stadium, Cardiff, in March 2008.

Right: The Argentina team line up for their National Anthem before the World Cup quarter-final game against Scotland in October 2007.

Opposite: South Africa's captain, John Smit celebrates the winning of the World Cup in 2007. He is accompanied by President Thabo Mbeki. In the background is the French President, Nicolas Sarkozy.

In the Six Nations the spoils have been shared by Wales, a Grand Slam in 2008, Ireland, a first Grand Slam since 1945 in 2009, France, winners in 2010 and England, Six Nations winners in 2011. The results of the Northern Hemisphere sides against the Tri Nation sides in the last four years have been poor. England managed to beat Australia in Sydney in June 2010 and again at Twickenham in November 2010, but they lost to New Zealand and South Africa at Twickenham. The only other successes of the Northern Hemisphere countries against the three giants of the south since the 2007 World Cup have been a dramatic win by France against New Zealand in Dunedin in 2009 by 27-20 and Scotland beating South Africa at Murrayfield in November 2010.

The form of the other countries in the tournament is not easy to assess for two reasons. Firstly, a number of sides, particularly the Pacific Islanders and Namibia play so few full Internationals. In 2009 Fiji, Tonga and Namibia played four each and Samoa played eight, although two of them were against Papua New Guinea. This compared with 14 played by New Zealand and Australia and 12 by South Africa and England.

Secondly, it is difficult for a number of countries to get their full squads together for Internationals outside the World Cup. Countries that suffer more than most are the Pacific Islanders and Argentina who are only able to get their full squads together every four years with so many of their players plying their trade in other countries.

The form book points to a New Zealand versus South Africa final, but when the knock-out stages begin at the quarter-finals any one of six teams will have the ability to beat any other side on the day. As has been shown on several occasions, Australia can beat the All Blacks and England has been able to peak at most World Cups, getting to three and winning one of the last five finals. They will be the side that no one wants to meet. The same could be said about France, although they have fallen at the last or penultimate hurdle in five of the six World Cups, losing in the semi-finals three times and the final twice.

After the heroics in 2007, Argentina cannot be left out of the equation. They need to get through their pool where they will face both England and Scotland, but, if they succeed, they will be dangerous competitors. They have some of the most experienced and talented players in the world and getting them all together for a training camp before the tournament will give them the belief that they can go further than their third place in 2007.

TEAMS

NEW ZEALAND

POOL A

New Zealand cannot wait for the start of the World Cup. Grant Fox, the legendary All Black fly half in the late 1980's and early 1990's, and scorer of 645 points in Tests during his career: "We're a little country down at the bottom of the world and this is one thing (playing rugby) that we do better than most and that makes us feel good about ourselves."

New Zealand must be favourites to win their second World Cup, 24 years after their first win. But, as Will Greenwood, the ex-England centre and World Cup winner in 2003, says, "They have an identity, they are the All Blacks and rugby is a serious business. In the past, this has cost them at World Cups. Their drive to be the best all the time has seen them peak at the wrong moment and make the wrong choices. This time round it seems as if they are getting it right. The only issue they have to deal with is that so are many of the other teams. The World Cup cycle is too well understood for coaches to make the same mistakes twice."

The expectation from the New Zealand public for their side to win for the first time since 1987 is overwhelming. Nothing short of seeing the New Zealand captain, Richie McCaw, lifting the Cup on Sunday, October 23rd will be satisfactory to most of the nation. The record since 1987 has been unacceptable for all those supporters who do not contemplate defeat. But defeat it has been for the All Blacks since the inaugural World Cup held jointly in Australia and New Zealand.

In 1991 they were beaten by Australia in the quarter-finals. A defeat in the 1995 final by the host nation, South Africa, was followed in 1999

Below: Joe Rokocoko passes the ball out wide, during the Investec Challenge match between England and New Zealand.

Fact File	
Captain	
Richie McCaw	
Star Player	
Dan Carter	
Top Try Scorer	
Doug Howlett (49)	
Current Most Capped Player	
Richie McCaw/Mils Muliaina	
Best Rugby World Cup Result	
Winner –1987	
Head Coach	
Graham Henry	

Left: Conrad Smith, the New Zealand centre, breaks through a tackle on the way to setting up another Kiwi try. Smith has been ever present in the side for the last few years, but now has competition from Sonny Bill Williams.

Below: Mils Muliaina scoring one of the many tries he has scored as an attacking full back. New Zealand has relied on his breaks from full back to breech defences and link up with either wing.

Previous spread: Australian players pose with the Trophy after the game in 1999 when they beat France at the Millennium Stadium, Cardiff.

by France staging an incredible fight-back in the second half to beat them in the semi-final at Twickenham. In 2003 they were well beaten by Australia in the semi-final and then in 2007 they unexpectedly lost to France in the quarter-final.

This would be considered a more than satisfactory record for most other countries but, with the 2011 tournament in New Zealand and the side having had mostly successful results against all the Tier 1 nations they have played since 2007, nothing less than winning the tournament will do.

They are top of the world rankings by some way and, in an extraordinary statement, the New Zealand Police have revealed that they are preparing for the risk of a surge in domestic violence if the All Blacks fail to win the World Cup.

In 1987 there was such confidence that the All Blacks would win that T-shirts bearing the legend, "Awesome All Blacks World Cup Winners 1987" were ordered months in advance.

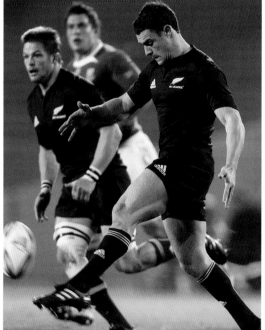

Above: Ben Franks, Keven Mealamu and Tony Woodcock forming the All Black front row against the Springboks in July 2010.
Right: Dan Carter, the super star fly half, kicks the ball to gain New Zealand valuable territory. Carter will be the key man in the Kiwi side and is considered to be the most complete fly half in the world.

Within minutes of David Kirk holding aloft the Cup, they were selling by the thousand. Will the marketing men take the same chance again?

With the other teams in Pool A, New Zealand should be able to rotate their squad to keep them fresh for the quarter-finals onwards.

One player does not make a team, but there is no doubt that the side is so much better with Dan Carter at outside half. Carter took off to France to play for Perpignan in the Top 14 competition in 2009 and New Zealand lost three of the six Internationals they played.

Carter returned after recovering from a ruptured Achilles tendon sustained playing in France and went back into the All Blacks side in January, helping them win two out of three of their remaining games.

They won all their games in the autumn tour of the Northern Hemisphere in 2010 with the only blemish being a 26-24 points defeat by Australia in Hong Kong en route to Europe.

The squad has a large amount of experience in Richie McCaw (the most capped All Black captain), Mils Muliaina, Dan Carter, Tony Woodcock and Keven Mealamu, backed up by newer players in Sonny Bill Williams, Owen Franks, Kieran Read, Hosea Gear and Sam Whitlock. The coaching team of Graham Henry, Steve Hansen and Wayne Smith is the most experienced in the business, so they are firm favourites to win on home soil.

It will take an outstanding performance to beat New Zealand, but then this has happened in five previous World Cups, so who will step up to the plate? The All Blacks will be wary of the French. As Andrew Mehrtens once said, "The French are predictably unpredictable".

Below: The New Zealand side celebrating another win in the build-up to the World Cup. They have been in stunning form since 2007 and desperately want to repeat the 1987 triumph when they beat France in their only World Cup win.

Right: Sonny Bill Williams on the attack during a Test match between New Zealand and Scotland at Murrayfield in November 2010.

New Zealand have had to keep their frustration from not winning since 1987 pent up and no longer want to hear the type of cutting remark by George Gregan, the then Australian captain, near the end of the semi-final win over the All Blacks in the 2003 World Cup. "Four more years, boys". A defeat in the quarter-finals in 2007 meant another four years – 2011 cannot come too soon for the land of the long white cloud.

New Zealand has world-class players across the team. They went 15 games without losing until they were beaten by Australia in the autumn of 2010. Players like Dan Carter, Richie McCaw, and Brad Thorn would get into any World XV. **Clockwise from top left:** Carter; McCaw, Thorn, Cory Jane, Ma'a Nonu.

FRANCE

POOL A

Rugby in France is riding high on a wave of enthusiasm, partly because of the decline of the national football side but also because of the interest in club rugby.

Also, if you want to maximise your income through your skill in rugby, France is the place to be at the moment. Rugby is the most popular game in many regions in the southern half of France and the players are treated in a similar way to footballers in other countries. They are paid very well, play in top stadiums, are involved in large squads (45 to 50 compared to 33 to 35 in Britain), so they get more rest. Spectator support is higher than anywhere else in Europe at most club games.

On this basis, France should have a large reservoir of players which should give the country a big advantage. But there is a hitch. Because of the wage structure where a top player can earn at least 40% more than his counterpart in Britain, there has been an influx of non-French players from literally all parts of the world. Britain and Ireland, South Africa, North and South America, Pacific Islands, Eastern Europe, Australia and New Zealand all have players with various French clubs. Many of the best players in the world are plying their trade in France and this has now got to the stage where the French Rugby Union has insisted on putting plans in place to reduce the number of overseas players playing in the French leagues and also to reduce the salary cap.

There is no doubt that the domestic competition in France has grown considerably in recent years with numerous games having "sold out" notices. Stade Français have now played a number of games at the Stade de France where they have attracted over 75,000 spectators for both league and Heineken Cup games.

The major national club competition in France is the Top 14 and the end of season play-off is an 80,000 sell-out. The vast majority of clubs and players reside in the southern half of France with the notable exception of the two major Paris clubs, Stade Français and Racing Metro.

Below: Sebastien Chabal, the dynamic number 8, is now back in France having spent five years in England playing for Sale. France wants to use him as a battering ram and it will be interesting to see if he starts or comes on as a second half replacement in the key games.

Fact File

Captain

Thierry Dusautoir

Star Player

Morgan Parra

Top Try Scorer

Serge Blanco (38)

Current Most Capped Player

Damian Traille

Best Rugby World Cup Result

2nd 1987, 1999

Head Coach

Marc Lievremont

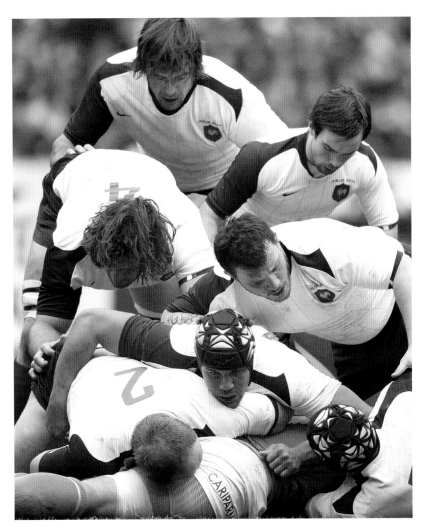

Top left and right: Thierry Dusautoir fights for the ball during the Six Nations tournament match between France and Italy; David Marty is congratulated by team mates after scoring a try against Fiji during the 2010 Autumn Internationals. **Below:** Thierry Dusautoir receiving the Six Nations Cup.

Above: Mathieu Bastareaud, the giant centre, who made an impact, in more ways than one, in action in the Six Nations Championship. Whether he makes the squad for the World Cup will depend on his form in the French Championship and his determination to get fit.

On the international front, Les Bleus became Six Nations Champions in 2010 with a Grand Slam win over England 12-10 in Paris. That followed on from a remarkable defeat of New Zealand in Dunedin, the first French success on Kiwi soil for 15 years. France has many outstanding players, but their problems have invariably appeared to stem from their selection process which has often bordered on the bizarre. Multiple changes, players selected out of position and combinations seeming to make no sense.

The latest coach is Marc Lievremont. He took over from Bernard Laporte who coached from 1999 to 2007. Lievremont has been eccentric in his selections, but in getting France success in the 2010 Six Nations Championship he combined the traditional Gallic flair and adventure with a certain amount of conservatism.

However, the wheels fell off in the Autumn Internationals of 2010 when they were humiliated by Australia 51 points to 16. Then in the Six Nations the inconsistent national side showed what they are – inconsistent. They beat Scotland and Ireland but lost to England at Twickenham and then surrendered in an abject manner to Italy in Rome.

A clear win against Wales in Paris in their last game probably saved Lievremont's job. But the knives are still out and he may not be there for the start of the World Cup.

France has never won the World Cup. They have reached the quarter-final stages of every tournament and have twice reached the final – in the first World Cup of 1987, being defeated by New Zealand, 29-9 at Eden Park in New Zealand, and in 1999 losing to Australia, 35-12 in Cardiff.

In 2007 they defeated New Zealand by 20-18 in the quarter-finals but then lost to England in Paris in the semi's by 14-9.

France will no doubt expect to get through to the quarter-finals, probably as runners-up to New Zealand. However, they are the one side that can spring a surprise, as witnessed in the epic semi-final in 1999 when they beat New Zealand, 43-31 in one of the most famous victories in World Cup history. So New Zealand will be very wary and will not take the French lightly in the pool game.

The captain Thierry Dusautoir, scrum half Morgan Parra, and Damien Traille are just three of their world-class International players – but which side will turn up in New Zealand? The destiny of the World Cup could be decided by the French.

Left: Imanol Harinordoquy in the back row is a dangerous runner for France, breaking from the scrum or in open play. He scored a try against Scotland in the Six Nations this year by sheer speed outpacing the defence. Competition for the back row places in the French side will be a feature of the World Cup.

Middle: Thierry Dusautoir, Nicolas Mas, William Servat, Thomas Domingo and Julien Pierre of France sing the National Anthem ahead of the RBS Six Nations Championship match between France and England.

Below: Morgan Parra will be in competition with Dimitri Yachvili for the scrum half spot. Both can kick goals and both can keep the pack going forward by kicking astutely from the base of the scrum. Parra has a lightning break and will expect to be first choice in the top games.

TONGA

POOL A

Rugby Union is the national sport of Tonga. For a country that has a total of 10,168 players (according to the official figures from the IRB), the fact that they compete with the Tier 1 Nations is an incredible achievement.

The main impetus for the establishment of rugby in Tonga came from the Irish missionaries in the 1920's who introduced it to the country's two main schools.

World class players, Jonah Lomu, Willie Ofahengaue, Toutai Kefu, Epi Taione and George Smith are all of Tongan descent.

Tonga has appeared in five of the previous World Cups. They did not record a victory in the 1987 tournament and missed out on qualification in 1991. They had one victory against the Ivory Coast in 1995 and then against Italy in 1999.

They lost all their games in 2003 but had their best results in the 2007 tournament in France when they beat USA and Samoa, as well as giving South Africa a massive fright before losing by 30 points to 25 in one of the most memorable games in the tournament.

The Tongan national team is nicknamed Ikale Tahi (Sea Eagles).

Like the other big Pacific rugby nations, Tonga has a pre-match ritual. The Sipi Tau is a form of Kailao, which was originally a war dance that was imported to Tonga from Wallis Island.

One of the most memorable performances in modern times of the Sipi Tau was during the 2003 World Cup in Australia. Tonga played the All Blacks who began their traditional Haka, and then Tonga answered to the Haka through the Sipi Tau,

Below left and right: Pierre Hola of Tonga converts a penalty against Samoa in the 2007 World Cup and Tonga's flanker Viliami Vaki runs to score a try during the 2007 World Cup Group A match between USA and Tonga.

Fact File

Captain

Aleki Lutui

Star Player

Pierre Hola

Top Try Scorer

Siva Taumallolo (12)

Current Most Capped Player

Pierre Hola

Best Rugby World Cup Result

3rd in Pool 1995 & 2007

Head Coach

Isitolo Maka

bringing the teams within almost touching distance just prior to kick-off.

Many of their players play in every corner of the world where rugby is played. They suffer from playing so few Internationals and really only have a chance of getting their top players together for the World Cup every four years.

If they can assemble all their top players based overseas, they will be very competitive. Players like lock Emosi Kauhenga, flanker Finau Maka and Captain Aleki Lutui plus relative newcomers, wings Mateo Malupo and William Helu, have the chance to shine in New Zealand.

It could be the best World Cup in the history of Tonga.

The forwards want to run with the ball on every opportunity, so they will hope for dry conditions – not generally guaranteed in New Zealand. However, they will want to get the ball away from the pack as quickly as possible and not get caught up in a forward battle.

Top: Finau Maka keeping the ball close to the other forwards.
Middle: Sione Mone Tu'ipulotu breaks from the scrum.
Bottom: The Tongans have their own traditional ritual, the Sipi Tau which they perform before every game, similar to the Haka performed by the All Blacks.

CANADA

Canada have competed in every World Cup to date, but have avoided defeat in only one match in each tournament with the exception of 1991 when they reached the quarter-finals. They managed to beat Tonga in 1987, Romania in 1995, Namibia in 1999 and Tonga again in 2003 with a draw against Japan in 2007. In 1991 they beat Fiji and Romania before narrowly losing 19-13 to France, but did enough to get to the quarter-finals where they lost to New Zealand by 29-13.

They are always a very competitive side, but suffer because of the sheer size of the country which has made inter-provincial competition difficult. Also, because of the climate it is impossible to play at certain times of the year and that leads to a split season.

In the past Canada was not short of international competition, as the antipodean sides often stopped off there before heading onto Europe. Similarly, Northern Hemisphere sides did the same, going in the opposite direction. However, this does not now occur and Canada have to make do with the yearly Churchill Cup where they play against the second-string sides of Tier 1 countries and emerging countries, such as Georgia and Russia.

Canada have not always lived up to the critics' view that they should be potential giant-killers and they are in a particular strong pool in 2011 with New Zealand, France, and threats coming from Tonga and Japan.

The Canadian coach is New Zealander, Kieran Crowley, who played in a pool game for the All Blacks in the 1987 World Cup. Crowley was appointed in 2008 with the job of seeing Canada getting through to the 2011 finals. They had a first-leg defeat by the USA in the qualifying round, but then recorded a comfortable 41-18 victory to secure their place in Pool A. Crowley was satisfied with the result, but warned, "We need to learn how to win games. We have stayed in against teams a lot better than us, but not quite finished off. It's pleasing to have Japan (in the World Cup), they are around about us, but you want to play a couple above you."

Canada has been helped on the international scene by the implementation of the Churchill Cup set up in 2003, a tournament held on alternative years in Canada and the USA. It is being held in England in 2011 It gives Canada an opportunity to play against a range of opposition that has included England Saxons, Ireland 'A', the New Zealand Maori, USA, Russia, Georgia and the Argentina Jaguars. Canada now benefit from being in the American Rugby Championship, launched in 2009, which includes four Canadian teams.

Many of the players are plying their trade abroad, mainly in Britain. Players like Aaron Carpenter (number 8) playing at Plymouth Albion along with Sean-Michael Stephen and Tyler Hotson. Glasgow also have Daniel Tailliferre Hauman van der Merwe, and Kevin Tkachuk. There is also the aggressive Jamie Cudmore at Clermont Auvergne.

Canada will do very well to get out of the pool. In fact, they will probably consider their campaign successful if they beat Japan and Tonga.

Below: Phil Mackenzie of Esher and Canada is tackled by England's Ty Shannon during a quarter-final Bowl match during the New Zealand International Sevens, 2008.

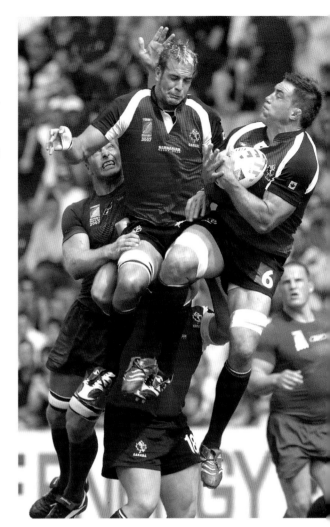

Left: Craig Culpan of Canada is tackled short of the try line by Martyn Williams of Wales during the 2007 Rugby World Cup.
Right: Canada's lock Jamie Cudmore and Luke Tait jump to grab the ball during the 2007 Rugby World Cup match against Wales.
Below: Bedford Blues' James Pritchard runs for a try in the Barclays Churchill Cup match between Canada and USA in 2006.

Fact File

Captain

Pat Riordan

Star Player

Aaron Carpenter

Top Try Scorer

Winston Stanley (24)

Current Most Capped Player

Kevin Tkachuk

Best Rugby World Cup Result

Quarter Finals 1991

Head Coach

Kieran Crowley

JAPAN

Japan starts with a major disadvantage in as much as they do not possess forwards capable of matching the giant packs of most rugby nations. However, as they have shown in previous World Cups, even playing with less than 30% possession, their backs can create tries with exciting running plays.
Below: Players like Takashi Kikutani are outstanding athletes.

Japan is a proud rugby nation. Rugby has been in existence for well over 100 years in the Far East. The British were responsible for taking the game to Japan and the Japanese Rugby Union was formed in 1926. The Second World War took its toll on the development of the game when pitches were dug up, and it was not until the 1950's that the game developed with visits by Oxford and Cambridge Universities, followed by Australian universities and New Zealand U 23 XV's.

Japan has appeared in all six previous World Cups, but can only point to one victory (against Zimbabwe in 1991) and a draw with Canada in 2007 as their best achievements.

Their coach is John Kirwan, who played in the winning New Zealand side in the first World Cup. Kirwan realised soon after arrival in Japan that the expectation of the nation had not been met and announced that, "We want to be the world's fittest team". He saw the strengths of the side as speed and agility, playing rugby that the big men don't like.

Kirwan has shown that he is his own man when preparing teams for international rugby: "Perhaps the most important lesson of all to learn is that trying to prepare too much can actually be a disservice. Can you really prepare for what is going to unfurl at a World Cup?"

"Italy showed that you cannot rely on experience alone. You need the input of youth as well to give the side some energy. The most important thing as a coach is to make sure the players are excited and keen to play. We have nothing to lose. We hope to win two of our four pool games. Anything else will be a bonus".

Japan have shown that they can score spectacular tries, but do not win enough ball and

Fact File

Captain

Takashi Kikutani

Star Player

Takashi Kikutani

Top Try Scorer

Daisuke Ohata

Current Most Capped Player

Hirotoki Onozawa

Best Rugby World Cup Result

3rd in Pool 1991

Head Coach

John Kirwan

still do not have the forwards to compete against the major nations.

In the last two years Japanese rugby has had to sort out various problems off the field. Toshiba Brave Lupus pulled out of the All-Japan Championship, having seen one of their players arrested for robbing a taxi driver and then Christian Loamanu tested positive for marijuana following a league game against Suntory Sungoliath. But the future now looks very bright for Japanese rugby. Although they were beaten by New Zealand in the vote for hosting the 2011 tournament, they achieved their ambition when they were awarded the 2019 World Cup.

"Japan has much to offer the Rugby World Cup. We have a superb transport system, strong infrastructure and world-class stadiums", Japan RFU president, Yoshiro Mori said.

For the 2011 World Cup Japan has a young and talented captain, Takashi Kikutani, and will hope to at least have their best World Cup to date.

Opposite right: The Japanese team celebrate winning in the men's gold medal match of rugby at University Town Main Stadium during day eleven of the 16th Asian Games on 23 November, 2010 in Guangzhou, China.

Above: Players from the Japan team pose with the trophy after winning the HSBC Asian Five Nations match between Japan and Hong Kong at Prince Chichibu Stadium on 22 May, 2010 in Tokyo, Japan.

Top: Members of the Japanese team prepare to pack down for the scrum during the HSBC Asian Five Nations match between Japan and Hong Kong, 2010.

ARGENTINA

POOL B

Argentina has several world-class players and a back division that has already shown in the 2007 World Cup that they can live with any opposition.

Below: Juan Martin Hernandez has troubled many opponents and Argentina will hope to repeat their heroics of the last World Cup when they beat France twice, in the pool stage and then in the third place play-off game.

Argentina had a wonderful 2007 World Cup. They had played in the previous five World Cups, coming third in their pool in 1999 and famously beating Ireland in a play-off for a quarter-final place, but losing to France in the quarter-final. They failed to get through the pool to the quarter-finals in 2003, but 2007 was their year. They topped the pool, beating France in the first game of the tournament and then went undefeated in the other pool games, beating Georgia (33-3), Namibia (63-3) and Ireland by 30 points to 15.

This meant they contested a quarter-final against Scotland. They triumphed in a tight game by 19 points to 13 and finally lost in the semi-final to South Africa by 37-13. But they were not finished, as they went on to meet and beat France for the bronze medal position. They won for the second time against France by 34-10.

Argentina came of age in the sixth World Cup and showed what most of those who had watched them over the last 10 years knew – that if only they could get all their best players training together for a length of time, then they had enough world-class players to challenge any of the top teams.

Those who had watched the Argentine players in Britain and France knew the quality was there, but it was often impossible to get all their top players assembled together. The World Cup gave that chance and the third place in the 2007 World Cup was the result. The catalyst for their success was arguably their 25-18 win over England in November 2008, Argentina's first victory at Twickenham.

Although football is the national game in Argentina, there is no denying the appeal of rugby to a large group of the population. The Academy Director and former England outside half (not well known to the punters) Les Cusworth, is very optimistic about Argentinian rugby, "Although there is no professional structure in Argentina, the enthusiasm and commitment is incredible. There is one team in Buenos Aires that attracts 1,300 children for training on a Sunday morning."

But, because there is no fully-professional rugby in Argentina, many players head towards the major playing countries as soon as they get a sniff of a professional contract. It is estimated that

Fact File

Captain

Felipe Contepomi

Star Player

Felipe Contepomi

Top Try Scorer

Jose Maria Nunez Piossek (29)

Current Most Capped Player

Mario Ledesma

Best Rugby World Cup Result

3rd 2007

Head Coach

Santiago Phelan

400 of Argentina's rugby-playing population are playing either professional or semi-professional rugby across Europe.

Argentina has now been invited by SANZAR to join a revamped Four Nations from 2012. Their problem in the past has been lack of international competition. Whereas the Tier 1 nations play a minimum of ten Test matches in a year, Argentina has found it difficult to find opponents for half that number. In the Four Nations they will overcome that issue.

Argentina 'A', now renamed the Jaguars, is a team selected from players still playing rugby in Argentina and can be considered to be the second-best team in the Americas, (behind their full national side), having beaten both the USA and Canada in the 2009 Churchill Cup.

The interesting issue is whether there will be a return of players to Argentina. The lure of a Four Nations tournament will be a factor. There is no professional league in Argentina and Los Pumas have got to address the issue to attract their stars back.

Felipe Contepomi, Gonzalo Tiesi, Juan Fernandez Lobbe, Rodrigo Roncero and Mario Ledesma are seasoned internationals playing overseas and have been joined by new boys like Gonzalo Camacho.

In 2011 they are in the same pool as England, Scotland, Georgia and Romania. They must fancy their chances of getting through to at least the quarter-finals by finishing in the top two in their pool. Neither Scotland nor England will consider the Argentine game as anything other than a full-blooded contest where any lack of concentration or commitment will be punished and either country could be on the end of a defeat and an early exit from the tournament.

Argentina have blooded new players like Gonzalo Camacho **(seen above beating Chris Robshaw)** when Argentina played England in 2009. These new players brought into the side, showing a wealth of experience, include Rodrigo Roncero, Mario Ledesma, Lucas Amorosino, Patricio Albacete and Gonzalo Tiesi **(middle).** For the World Cup they will be able to call on all their stars that play abroad. Under the captaincy of Felipe Contepomi, the backs will be provided with the platform to win matches. They will, however, have to play even better than in 2007 because the opposition will be waiting for them this time around.

Argentina will prove difficult opponents to the two British sides, England and Scotland in Pool B, and it will be no surprise if they get out of the pool at the expense of one of the favoured sides and advance to the quarter-finals. They need to keep free of injuries to their players and keep their composure under pressure.

Clockwise from top left: Lucas Gonzalez Amorosino, Juan Manuel Leguizamon, Felipe Contepomi, Patricio Albacete and Rafael Carballo.

ENGLAND

Martin Johnson, the England manager, has had to learn a number of hard lessons in the last two years, but now has a squad that blends youth with experience.

England could be the side no-one wants to meet in this year's World Cup.

Critics derided their form in 2006 and there was good reason for even the most ardent of English supporters to think 2007 would not be a good year for the team. Not just indifferent form in the Six Nations and the thrashing at the hands of Australia and New Zealand Down Under but, then in a pool game, a morale-sapping loss to South Africa where they were taken to the cleaners, losing 34-0. Most thought they would drop out at the quarter-final stage, but instead they beat the hot favourites Australia in Marseilles in the quarter-final and then took on the hosts, France, in the cauldron of the Stade de France in Paris in the semi-final and secured a famous victory.

Three weeks later, the same side met South Africa again in the final and they lost by 15 points to 6 in a game where they had a try disallowed and could easily have won.

Only two countries have played back-to-back finals – Australia did in 1999 (winners) and 2003 (runners-up), and England repeated this in 2003 (winners) and 2007 (runners-up). Only Australia and England have played in three finals and that is why it would be foolish to bet against either of them in 2011.

But England has had a difficult time since 2007. They dispensed with two coaches, Brian Ashton, who had taken over from Andy Robinson, and failed to win the Six Nations or even a Triple Crown. Martin Johnson has had his problems and critics since he took over from Brian Ashton. There was a chink of light when England defeated Australia during their 2010 summer tour of Australia and New Zealand, the first success after nine successive defeats to

Fact File

Captain

Lewis Moody

Star Player

Toby Flood

Top Try Scorer

Rory Underwood (49)

Current Most Capped Player

Joe Worsley/Jonny Wilkinson

Best Rugby World Cup Result

Winner 2003

Head Coach

Martin Johnson

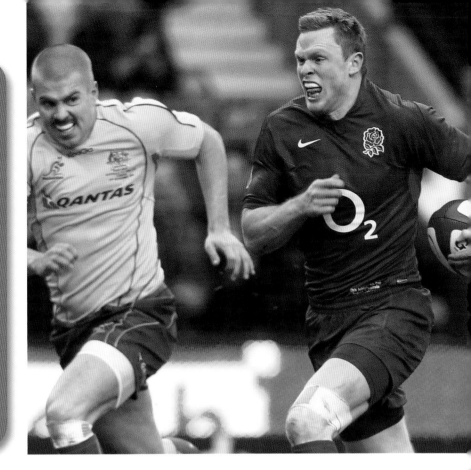

Above right: Chris Ashton is now one of the most exciting players in world rugby. A prolific try scorer, Ashton is a Rugby League convert and one of the aces in Johnson's team.

Right: Another very exciting player to hit the international scene in the last 12 months is Ben Youngs, the England scrum half. He has an eye for even the smallest of openings and an electric break. England will expect him to galvanise the team.

Two other players who will be key to England's hopes are Tom Croft in the back row **(below left)** and Toby Flood **(below right)**, the outside half who has taken over from Jonny Wilkinson. Flood, in particular, could determine the outcome of tight games with his decision-making and goal-kicking.

Right: Ben Foden catches a high ball against Australia in the Cook Cup Test Match, 2010.

Australia, and then in the Autumn Internationals in 2010 they comprehensively defeated Australia at Twickenham, although losing to both New Zealand and South Africa. But it was the manner by which they played that brought hope for the supporters. And it all started to come together with the 2011 Six Nations until they fell to earth in Dublin in their last game of the tournament. They needed to beat Ireland to win the Grand Slam but they lost comprehensively and it showed that there is no substitute for experience which is not in abundance in this young England side.

In Martin Johnson, although having no formal official coaching experience, there is faith that he will bring the team to New Zealand in the right shape, peaking at the right time.

The side is young with a large pack featuring the dynamic Tom Croft, Tom Palmer and the ever-improving Dan Cole. It now has some exciting backs with Ben Foden, Chris Ashton and Ben Youngs as match winners, if given a fair share of the ball.

In their pool they have both Scotland and Argentina to beat to get to the quarter-finals, both potential banana skins, but England have shown they can peak at the right time, as they did in 2003 and 2007.

The England pack (top right) will not be the most experienced in the tournament, but in Andrew Sheridan, Nick Easter (bottom right) and Lewis Moody they have campaigners that have played in previous World Cups and will be backed up by the younger players like Croft, Dylan Hartley (right), Dan Cole and James Haskell who have shown they can mix it with the rest. The emergence of Courtney Lawes and Alex Corbisiero means that England will hold their own in a forwards battle.

England has a settled side with good replacements in certain positions sitting in the wings, hoping for a chance. Possibly the only contentious area is the mid-field where an ageing Mike Tindall has been partnering Shontayne Hape, with Toby Flood occupying the outside half position. There are options in all these positions with Ricky Flutey back from injury, Jonny Wilkinson strutting his stuff in France with Toulon and Delon Armitage and Matt Banahan, both able to play in more than one position.

Hooker, back row, scrum half and props are all covered with good replacements, so England will not be short of back-up if injuries occur. They certainly cannot be written off for a semi-final place, although they would love to go into the tournament as one of the underdogs.

SCOTLAND

POOL B

Apart from reaching the semi-final in 1991 where they lost a very fraught game by 9 points to 6 against England, Scotland have won through the pool stages in all the other five tournaments, but lost on all five occasions in the quarter-finals.

They are in the same pool as England, Argentina, Georgia and Romania. Pool B is not an easy pool, with both England and Argentina ahead of Scotland in the world rankings. But Scotland have a new-found belief under coach Andy Robinson and they will expect to get through to the quarter-finals at the expense of one of the other two.

Robinson had led Edinburgh to second place in the Magners League. In an upbeat mood, he said he was confident that he can take the players and the national team onto bigger and better things. "I believe we have a crop of players who can really challenge the world's best."

The advent of professionalism in the mid-1990's was not greeted with acclaim north of the border, the Scottish Rugby Union deciding that the existing club system operating in the Scottish leagues was not competitive enough. After a spell using District teams (effectively select teams drawing together the best amateur players from clubs in a given area), the SRU decided to create professional clubs to compete in the Celtic League (which became the Magners League). They started with four teams. However, these proved a disaster in European competition and the number was cut down to three. But financial constraints has meant that the Scottish fully-professional sides are just two, Glasgow and Edinburgh.

They are more competitive than previous Scottish sides but have yet to make a real impact on the cross-border competition, the Heineken Cup.

The national side is chosen almost exclusively from these two sides, but there are now several Scottish internationals playing outside Scotland, including Sean Lamont at Scarlets and Kelly Brown at Cardiff Blues. They have a world-class full back in Chris Paterson whose goal kicking is as good as anyone in world rugby.

Previous page: Martin Johnson and Jonny Wilkinson holding the William Webb Ellis Trophy won by England in 2003 in Sydney, Australia.

Below: Scotland flanker Kelly Brown runs clear of Welsh lock Alun-Wyn Jones during the RBS Six Nations International match between Wales and Scotland, 2010.

Fact File

Captain

Alastair Kellock

Star Player

Richie Gray

Top Try Scorer

I. S. Smith (24)

Current Most Capped Player

Chris Paterson

Best Rugby World Cup Result

4th 1991

Head Coach

Andy Robinson

They have two good scrum halves in Mike Blair and Rory Lawson, competitive forwards Richie Gray, Nathan Hines, Euan Murray and captain Alastair Kellock plus astute three quarters in Max Evans and Joe Ambro, but Scotland finds it difficult to regularly fill Murrayfield apart from some of the Six Nations games. However, Andy Robinson has had his successes. England scrambled a draw in Edinburgh in 2010 and Scotland had a moment of glory when they deservedly beat the World Champions, South Africa, last November. They had their one solitary win against Italy in the 2011 Six Nations but were competetive in all their other games.

Scotland are not in an easy pool and some supporters will feel they have a result if they get through to the quarter-finals which means that they will almost certainly have to beat either England or Argentina to achieve this.

Left: Max Evans in action during the RBS Six Nations Championship match between Scotland and France, 2010.

Above: Chris Paterson of Scotland kicks a penalty in the same match.

Below: Sean Lamont powers through the Irish defence during the RBS Six Nations match between Ireland and Scotland, 2010.

Above: Nathan Hines charges into contact with Jimmy Cowan of the All Blacks during the Test match between New Zealand and Scotland at Murrayfield Stadium on 13 November, 2010.

Right: Dan Park scores a drop goal against Wales during Six Nations in 2010. His tactical kicking has been instrumental in gaining valuable territory.

Opposite above: Scotland scrum half Chris Cusiter clears the ball during the RBS Six Nations International match between Wales and Scotland, 2010.

Opposite below: Scottish players celebrate at the end of the Test match against Argentina, 19 June, 2010.

GEORGIA

This will be the third time that Georgia has won their right to join the finals of the World Cup. The Lelos, as they are known, arrived in Australia in 2003, full of hope but not knowing how they would perform. They were in the same pool as South Africa, England, Uruguay and Samoa.

Disappointingly, they lost all their pool games and suffered their heaviest-ever defeat when beaten by England 84-6 in their opening game and lost their other three games.

They learnt from that experience and in 2007 they performed strongly, particularly in their game against Ireland which included a disallowed try, three drop goals and Georgia spending the last five minutes just metres from the Irish line – they lost by 14 points to 10. They did secure their first World Cup win with a convincing 30-0 victory over Namibia.

In the 2011 tournament they are in Pool B with Argentina, Scotland, England, and Romania, and will expect at least one win.

A majority of the squad play in France including scrum half Iraki Abuseridze (Auxerre), lock Mamuka Gorgodze (Montpellier), Davit Ziiakashuili (Clermont) and Levan Datunashvili (Figeac). They have players at Brive, Montauban, Toulon, Castres and Agen but they do not get that much match time in the first team and there are a number of other players based in the lower divisions. However, this situation is improving for Georgia. The team has at least nine of the 28 players in the recent squad based at home with the top five clubs, RC AIA, Lelo, Locomotive, Kochebi, and Universteti.

Rugby Union has become one of the most popular sports in Georgia, especially in the south of the country where it is more popular than soccer. When Georgia played Russia in the European Nations Cup, 65,000 watched at the national stadium in Tbilisi, with Georgia winning 17-13. Georgia has only 4.2 million inhabitants but has had crowds in excess of 12,000 per game for home matches of the Lelos.

There are 41 clubs with around 4,000 registered players. Rugby is certainly on the rise across the country with the national government being very supportive, incorporating a special four-year support programme that has helped to spread the game outside Tbilisi.

Their coach, the much travelled Richie Dixon worked with the 1999 World Champions, Australia, and also with the Springboks. He has proved to be an inspirational coach for a group of players always willing to learn. The rugby followers in Georgia will expect a lot from their team, but one win against Romania might be all they can achieve.

Below: Georgia's players sing their National Anthem before the World Cup Group D match against Argentina, 2007.

Top left: Merab Kvirikashvili takes a drop out against Namibia in September 2007.

Top right: Davir Katcharava breaks away to score in a game against Namibia.

Above: Goderdzi Shvelidze tries to break through the Spanish defence during the qualifying match in Tbilisi in February 2010.

ROMANIA

POOL B

In spite of the fact that Romanian rugby went through a total rebuilding process following the upheaval of 1989, they have succeeded in qualifying for all the World Cups and won through to this year's finals by beating Uruguay to the last place. Their ambition will be to be as competitive as possible, hoping to achieve one victory in the process.
Below: Ovidiu Tonita looks on.
Below right: Manta Alexandru with the ball.

Romania was the last side to be confirmed as qualifying for the final stages of the World Cup. They had to play Uruguay for the final spot in a two-legged home and away tie. The game was drawn 21 points each in Montevideo before Romania convincingly won in Bucharest by 39-12. This gave them entry into Pool B with Argentina, England, Scotland and Georgia.

Romania has played in all the previous World Cups, winning one pool game in each tournament, apart from 1995 when they lost all their games. For a country that had to completely rebuild its rugby structure after the 1989 revolution where it saw several leading players lose their lives, including the Romanian captain, Florica Murariu, who was shot dead at a roadblock, it is one of only twelve teams who will have competed in all World Cups since 1987.

Romania had long been considered one of the strongest European teams outside of the Six Nations and currently competes in the First Division of the European Nations Cup. However,

the likes of Georgia and now Russia, will challenge Romania in the future for the top spot.

The irony of the situation for Romania was that during pre-professionalism, Romanian players were more professional than in most other countries, as their squad was made up of players from the two top clubs, Dynamo Bucharest (police side) and Steau Bucharest (army side), who were given whatever time was required for playing and training as well as being paid in the 'nominal' jobs.

The advent of legitimate professionalism in the game in 1995 spelt disaster for Romania. There was a massive exodus of players overseas, mainly to France, and a whole generation of potential referees and administrators were lost to the game. It took until the mid-2000's for Romania to get their act together and become really competitive again.

Half of the squad is playing in Romania but they have their captain, Sorin Socul, flanker, Ovidiu Tonita and fly half Iulian Dumitras, all playing in France. They will have to have all their players playing overseas to be available to have any chance of an upset.

Fact File

Captain

Sorin Socol

Star Player

Ovida Tonita

Top Try Scorer

Petre Motrescu (33)

Current Most Capped Player

Sorin Socol/Ovida Tonita

Best Rugby World Cup Result

3rd in Pool 1987, 1991, 1999

Head Coach

Steve McDowell

Romania, who were the strongest European side outside the Six Nations, now have strong competition from Russia and Georgia. Like all Eastern European countries, they have a large pack but lack the skills in the backs required at international level to penetrate well organised defences.

Left: Romania's players salute the crowd after their valiant loss at the Velodrome stadium in Marseilles, 2007.

Above: Romeo Gontineac fights off Sione Lauaki and Keith Robinson of New Zealand, Stadium de Toulouse, 2007.

AUSTRALIA

POOL C

Australia has a star-studded back line with Matt Giteau and Will Genia **(below left and right)** plus Kurtley Beale at full back, James O'Connor on one wing and Quade Cooper at fly half. A back line that is so exciting when all the parts function, as in November 2010 when Australia trounced France.

Australia has been the most successful side in the short history of the World Cup. They have been in three finals out of the six so far played and have won twice. South Africa has won both the finals in which they have played but have only played in four of the six World Cups.

For a country where Rugby Union is behind Aussies Rules, Rugby League and cricket as the people's favourite sport, the international team continue to produce star-quality players at an early age and they are not afraid to put them in the firing line.

The professional game in Australia is based on the teams that compete in the Investec Super 14. They are the Brumbies, Western Force, Queensland Reds, NSW Waratahs and these were joined in 2011 by Melbourne Rebels. There are very few non-Australian qualified players in these five sides, so the selectors have around 150 players from which to choose the national squad.

In the run-up to the 2003 World Cup Australia's form was indifferent, but they managed to get to the semi-final when they defeated the All Blacks by 22-10, one of their greatest victories. Their defeat

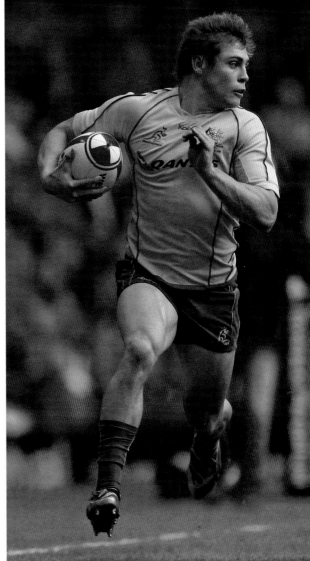

Fact File

Captain

Rocky Elsom

Star Player

Quade Cooper

Top Try Scorer

David Campese (64)

Current Most Capped Player

Nathan Sharpe/Matt Giteau

Best Rugby World Cup Result

Winner 1991 and 1999

Head Coach

Robbie Deans

Top left to bottom right:
Quade Cooper is a wonderful talent who never stops looking to unlock the tightest of defences; James O'Connor is a brilliant balanced runner who can also kick goals, whilst Kurtley Beale loves to come into the three-quarter line at every opportunity.

Right: On the other wing is Drew Mitchell, a busy player who scored four tries against France in the November 2010 game.

Below and opposite: In the forwards Nathan Sharpe and Rocky Elsom are the senior players. Elsom captains the side, having returned in 2009 from a spell in Ireland with Leinster, helping them win the Heineken Cup. The key for Australia will be the strength of their front row which has been their Achilles heel on some occasions in the past.

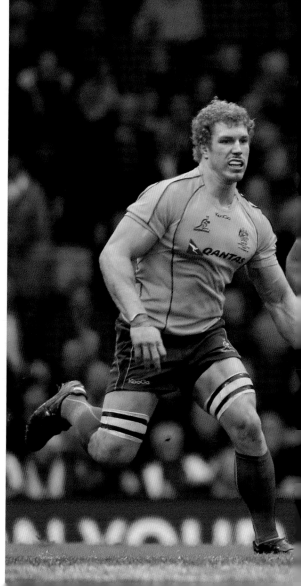

in the final against England was even more galling because it was on Australian soil and by an extra-time drop goal from Jonny Wilkinson who the Australian press had derided with comments like, "Is that all you've got", as Wilkinson was kicking England to victory in the earlier rounds.

When Australia lost to England in the quarter-finals in Marseilles in the 2007 World Cup, Eddie Jones resigned and Robbie Deans, an ex-New Zealand hooker took over as head coach.

They had mixed results, winning only seven of their 14 games in 2009, and the 2010 Tri Nations was not as successful as they would have planned. However, they had a morale-boosting win against New Zealand by 26-24 in Hong Kong on the way to Europe last October. They scored a try in overtime, which was converted in a nerveless fashion from the touchline by James O'Connor. O'Connor had also scored the try and this result ended a run of ten straight defeats for the Wallabies against the All Blacks. They lost to England in June 2010 and again in the Autumn Internationals, but secured a resounding victory against France by 59-16 in November, scoring 46 points in the second half. They ran France ragged and showed what an exciting back division could achieve, although the French were certainly missing in action in the second half.

To do what they have done in every other World Cup and get through to the quarter-finals they will have to beat at least three of their opponents in the pool games against Ireland, Italy, Russia and USA, with the Irish as the only real danger.

They certainly have the players. Youngsters like James O'Connor, Quade Cooper, Drew Mitchell, Will Genia and Adam Ashley-Cooper play alongside experienced players, Rocky Elsom, Matt Giteau and David Pocock. They are certainly capable of repeating what they have done before.

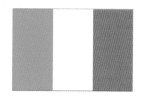

IRELAND

If there is one country that ought to have performed better in all the World Cups but has consistently failed, then it is Ireland. They have never got past the quarter-final stages and in the last World Cup they did not proceed beyond the pool stages.

They certainly have the players to do better. Most are chosen from three main Provincial sides, Munster, Leinster and Ulster which are continually in the top bracket of the successful sides in the Heineken Cup. The Irish sides have been in six finals of the Heineken Cup in the last 10 years and Munster has been a winner on two occasions.

So it is a mystery why the national team has not done better. They have always had world-class players in their ranks but losing four quarter-finals in six World Cups hardly puts them in the giant-killing category that they should be.

In his first season as Irish coach, Declan Kidney steered the side to their first Grand Slam for 61 years in the 2009 Six Nations Championship. Kidney had led the Munster side to four Heineken Cup finals in eight years and has now achieved the Holy Grail of a Six Nations Grand Slam.

Kidney was gracious enough to acknowledge the role played by his predecessor, Eddie O'Sullivan, who won three Championships but missed out on clean sweeps.

One of the problems for the Irish management is how long do they persevere with the ageing players who have done Ireland proud over the last 10 years. Tommy Bowe and Brian O'Driscoll are still match-winning players. Jamie Heaslip and David Wallace together with Paul O'Connell fortify a combative pack. These players have seen their Provincial sides win epic battles in the Heineken Cup. Can they continue for one more last hurrah or do Ireland have to put their faith in youth? Coach Kidney must weigh up Ronan O'Gara v Jonathan Sexton, Peter Stringer v Tomas O'Leary v Eion Reddan, Geordan Murphy v Rob Kearney v Keith Earls. Ireland's success will depend on his decisions.

They have the players but have not been able to win key World Cup games in the past. 2011 will test the players' resolve. Their form in the Six Nations typified their inconsistency. They were fortunate to beat Italy in their opening game, beat Scotland unconvincingly, but had losses to France and Wales. They then took on England in Dublin with the Grand Slam beckoning for England. England was favourite, but Ireland never gave England a chance and came out worthy winners by 24-8.

This is how they have got to play in the World Cup. 2011 could be the year that Ireland spring a surprise and become serious challengers for honours.

Below: Paul O'Connell will be playing in his last World Cup, as will a number of the Irish team who will want to improve on Irish shortcomings in previous World Cups.

Fact File

Captain

Brian O'Driscoll

Star Player

Tommy Bowe

Top Try Scorer

Brian O'Driscoll (43)

Current Most Capped Player

Brian O'Driscoll

Best Rugby World Cup Result

Quarter-Final 1987, 1991, 1995, 2003

Head Coach

Declan Kidney

Captain Brian O'Driscoll (**above**) will be key as will Tommy Bowe (**left**) and James Heaslip (**top**). They are in the same pool as Australia, but definitely ought to get through to the quarter-finals where they need some old Munster determination to win at all costs. They have the players, now they need the character to move on from the pool stages.

Opposite: Eoin Reddan passes the ball during the International Rugby Test match between New Zealand and Ireland at Yarrow Stadium, 2010.
Top: Keith Earls dives over the line to score a try during the RBS Six Nations match between England and Ireland at Twickenham Stadium, 2010.
Middle: Jonathan Sexton of Ireland is tackled by Matt Giteau during the Lansdowne Cup Test match between the Australian Wallabies and Ireland at Suncorp Stadium, Brisbane, Australia in 2010.
Bottom: David Wallace evades a tackle from Nick De Luca of Scotland during the RBS Six Nations match between Scotland and Ireland at Croke Park in Dublin, Ireland.

ITALY

Italy will have to rely on a number of established players like Mirco Bergamasco **(below right)** and Andrea Masi **(below)** putting in a world-class performance, if they are going to survive the pool stage.

Italy played in the first-ever World Cup match in 1987 in a match against the host nation, New Zealand. Unfortunately, the match proved a very one-sided affair with the All Blacks crushing Italy by 70 points to 6.

John Kirwan, who was the Italian national coach from 2002 until 2005, scored one of the greatest tries in the tournament's history.

Italy has appeared in every World Cup and they have had 7 wins out of the 20 games they have played. However, these wins have all been against countries in Tier 2 or below. Their most significant scalp was Argentina in 1995 when they beat them in a rousing game by 31 points to 25.

It was felt that, by entering the Five Nations Championship in 2000 to create the Six Nations, it would give Italy the boost it needed to compete on a more regular basis with the big boys of the Northern Hemisphere. They have had a few successes but have only won eight out of 60 games played in the competition up to 2011, so

it will be a long time before they get anywhere near winning a Six Nations Championship. However, they achieved a wonderful victory against France in March 2011which was as deserved as it was unexpected.

One of their problems has been that a number of their star players play in club competitions, mainly in England and France. However, with the entry of two sides into the Magners League from the 2010/11 season, this could gradually reverse the trend with more top players deciding to stay in Italy which should increase the competitiveness of the two main Italian sides and benefit the national side.

At the moment players like Sergio Parisse (Stade Français), Mirco Bergamasco (Racing Metro), Gonzalo Canale (Clermont), Andrea Masi (Racing Metro), Martin Castrogiovanni (Leicester) and Santiago Dellape (Racing Metro) all play abroad.

Italy has had some world-class players but not enough at any one time, so the national side has been short of class in many key positions.

Fact File

Captain

Sergio Parisse

Star Player

Sergio Parisse

Top Try Scorer

Marcello Cuttitta (25)

Current Most Capped Player

Andrea Lo Cicero

Best Rugby World Cup Result

Two wins; one in 2003 and one in 2007

Head Coach

Nick Mallett

Recently the lack of an international class scrum half and, to a lesser extent, outside half, has held them back in major games.

Italy has also had a succession of foreign coaches in the last ten years: Brad Johnstone (2000-2002), John Kirwan (2002-5), Pierre Berbizier (2005-7) and Nick Mallett, who has coached the side the last four years.

The entry of the two sides to play in the Magners League (Treviso and Aironi) has meant a downsizing of the domestic league to a semi-professional status which reduces costs to clubs that have been struggling to survive in a difficult economic climate. However, there have been signs that Italy are becoming more competitive, particularly since beating France 22-21 in the 2011 RBS Six Nations. The thrilling final five minutes were nail-biting for all.

Italy would hope to win at least two games in their pool, but both Russia and the USA will have their own ambitions, so it will not be easy for them to come out of the tournament feeling they have made progress.

Nick Mallett, Italy's coach, has made a plea about fixtures for the national side, "Italy rarely plays teams below them in the IRB rankings. More games against 'lesser' opposition would give Italy a chance to play with more ambition and freedom." We will see.

Top: Alessandro Zanni of Italy charges upfield during the RBS Six Nations match between Italy and England at Stadio Flaminio on 14 February, 2010.
Middle: Italy's flanker Mauro Bergamasco grabs the shorts of Wales' wing Shane Williams.
Bottom: Itay's scrum half Pablo Canavosio passes the ball during the Six Nations match against France, 14 March, 2010.

Above: Italy's captain, Sergio Patrisse is one of the world's best back row forwards, but he cannot work miracles. Italy lack an experienced pair of half backs and their defence can falter, allowing the opposition to move the ball around the field.

Left: Luciano Orquera taken down by Martin Scelzo of Argentina, 13 November, 2010.

Opposite: Italy have forwards that have gained considerable experience playing outside Italy, including Martin Castrogiovanni and Marco Bortolami, so they need to use this experience.

RUSSIA

The revolution in Russia is of the sporting type where an Englishman has guided the Russian national rugby side to the finals of the 2011 World Cup.

Steve Diamond, the former Sale and Saracens coach, was the motivator behind Russia's first time in the finals. He has been assisted by another Brit, Howard Thomas, executive vice president, who previously worked for Sale and Premiership Rugby. Diamond has been lured back to Sale to resurrect a club that has had a difficult time in the last two years.

The Rugby Union of the Soviet Union was, in fact, founded in 1936. They were not a major world force, unlike in other sports. They played as a Commonwealth of Independent States in matches during 1991 and 1992. In 1992 they became the Russian National Rugby Union team.

They qualify for their first World Cup. They were disqualified from the 2003 competition because they had three South African players who were not qualified to play for Russia. In 2007 RWC qualifying, they progressed steadily through the early qualifying rounds but their dream ended when they lost in Lisbon to Portugal by 26-23.

However, they have made considerable strides since and, under Steve Diamond's guidance, booked their place in the 2011 RWC with a draw against Romania at the end of February, 2010.

Russia have competed regularly in the European National Cup, and more recently, in the IRB Nations Cup. They were invited to participate in the Churchill Cup in America in 2010 and, although they did not win any of their games, they gained very valuable experience.

Russia toured New Zealand in January 2011 for an extended training camp as well as playing games against a Taranaki International XV and South Canterbury. They won both games by 33-24 and 31-7. In Februay and March they played in the European Nations Tournament, taking on Georgia, Romania and Spain.

More than 20,000 people now play the game, with vital backing from the president of the RRU, Russian billionaire, Vyacheslav Kopier. Kopier has played rugby since he was a student and in 2003

Below: Victor Gresev runs in for a try against Uruguay during the Churchill Cup match in June 2010.

Fact File

Captain

Vladislav Korshunov

Star Player

Artemyev Vasily Artemiev

Top Try Scorer

Viatcheslav Grachev

Current Most Capped Player

Andrey Kuzin

Best Rugby World Cup Result

Third in pool in 1991

Head Coach

Nikolay Nerush/Kingsley Jones

was elected president of the Rugby Union of Russia. In 2004 he was elected vice president of FIRA-AER.

Steve Diamond is full of praise for what has happened, "To get to the World Cup finals is a fantastic achievement and is the result of two years of incredibly hard work. The next target is to have 50,000 players in 5 years. I believe that's possible. Once Russia gets a taste for something it really goes for it – getting to the World Cup will undoubtedly help Russia move to the next level".

Russia is in the same pool as Italy, Ireland, Australia and the USA. A game of rugby against America will be something that most rugby followers will not want to miss.

Clockwise from top: Vladimir Ostroushko breaks through a tackle during a match against South Canterbury in Timaru, New Zealand, during a short tour by Russia in January 2010; Argentina in a friendly which gave Russia valuable experience for the World Cup; Russia celebrate after defeating Uruguay 38-19 to win the Bowl Final in the Churchill Cup; Victor Gresey tackles Ivo Dugonjic of Uruguay during the Churchill Cup in June, 2010.

USA

USA has suffered in recent years from a coaching roundabout with three coaches in four seasons. The Australian-born coach, Scott Johnson, wanted to put his faith in youth, declaring that he could develop a number of 20-year-olds into internationals.

The problem was that Johnson jumped ship to become Director of Rugby at Ospreys and the former Ireland coach, Eddie O'Sullivan, who had been an assistant coach to the USA in 1999, became the new coach.

In qualifying for the 2011 World Cup they had home and away fixtures against Canada. They won the first game 12-6, but a poor first half in the return fixture in Edmonton dashed their hope of qualifying ahead of Canada. They did eventually qualify by beating Uruguay to end up in Pool C.

There is new-found optimism in America with the new Americas Rugby Championship involving four Canadian provinces, the Argentina Jaguars and a USA select side. High-performance programmes are in place to develop young talent, particularly via the University teams and several players are making a big impression in the major rugby-playing countries overseas. Todd Clever is playing for the Lions in South Africa, Chris Wyles is at Saracens and Takudzwa Ngwenya, the flying wing, is playing at Biarritz.

Although Rugby Union still occupies a small but growing place in American sport, the potential for development is immense. Television coverage, particularly via ESPN, which shows live Tests, and ABC featuring highlight shows of the USA Sevens, is helping to popularise the game. However, the problems of distance to travel, climatic variations, restrictions because of funding, do not help, but the States has an enormous number of athletes who have the size and speed that are needed to succeed in rugby. A telling quote by the Eagles Sevens coach summed up the potential that, if tapped properly, could revolutionise the fortunes of USA rugby. "When we train at the Olympic training centre they have a big database where an athlete can type in 'I run the 100 metres in 10.2 seconds, but I didn't qualify for the Olympics, I weigh this much. What other sports can I play?' I've found over

Below left and right: Chris Wyles, who can play on the wing or full back is a key player for the Eagles. He plays regularly for the Saracens in the English Premiership; Scrum half Chad Erskine clears the ball from a ruck during a World Cup match against Samoa in September 2007.

a thousand athletes that can run 10.2 seconds at one hundred metres and weigh over 91kg. I don't know if they can catch and pass yet, but if they can see the atmosphere at a Wellington, a Dubai or a Hong Kong Sevens, and we can attract those types of athletes, then we can continue to promote the sport in the United States".

In the 2007 World Cup, the Eagles acquitted themselves very well with strong performances against England and South Africa. They scored a spectacular try through their Zimbabwean-born wing, Takudzwa Ngwenya, against South Africa, which won the Try of the Year in the IRB Awards. Ngwenya outpaced the Springbok flyer, Bryan Habana, and now plies his trade in France.

USA will seek to win at least two games and go home feeling they have competed to the best of their ability.

From top to bottom: Philip Eloff gets past Alesana Tuilagi of Samoa in a World Cup game; Louis Stanfill beats Tonga's fly half Pierre Hola during a World Cup match in Montpellier, France in September 2007; Veteran fly half Marcus Hercus attempts to beat the Tongan defence in the same match.

Fact File

Captain

Todd Clever

Star Player

Takudzwa Ngwenya

Top Try Scorer

Vaea Anitoni (26)

Current Most Capped Player

Mike MacDonald

Best Rugby World Cup Result

one win in 1987 and one in 2003

Head Coach

Eddie O'Sullivan

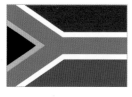

SOUTH AFRICA

South Africa arrives in New Zealand as reigning World Champions, determined to be the first side to successfully defend the title. Their desire to win will be even more focused because they will be in the backyard of their most attritional opponent and will find it even more pleasurable to win on New Zealand soil.

The Springboks did not play in the 1987 and 1991 tournaments because of the apartheid issues, but won in 1995 in front of their biggest supporter, Nelson Mandela, and had a second win in 2007, defeating England in the final.

Since then they have had mixed fortunes. They appointed Peter de Villiers as the first ever non-white coach and in 2008 had a disappointing Tri Nations, ending with only two wins. Then the 2009 season began very successfully with a 2-1 Test series win over the Lions. They followed this up with a convincing win in the Tri Nations sweeping aside the All Blacks and losing only one game out of six played in the tournament to the Wallabies in

Brisbane. In the second Test against the Kiwis which the Springboks won by 31-19, Morne Steyn set a number of records by scoring all South Africa's points – 1 try, 1conversion and 8 penalties. But in November they lost to France and surrendered their top world ranking.

In 2010 they went to Cardiff to play a one-off game against Wales in June and won 34-31 in spite of not having six front line players available. They then played two Internationals against Italy in South Africa which they won with ease. But in the Tri Nations they had a disastrous tournament, losing to both New Zealand and Australia thereby slipping below Australia in the world ranking.

In their tour of the Northern Hemisphere in the autumn of 2010 they unexpectedly lost to Scotland but comprehensively defeated England, after England had put Australia to the sword two weeks earlier.

They have quality players all over the field. Victor Matfield has entered the centenary club for

Below left and right: John Smit gets past Dean Munn of Australia during a Tri Nations game in July 2010; Ruan Pienaar could be a key figure for South Africa, as he showed against the British Lions in 2009.

Fact File

Captain

John Smit/Victor Matfield

Star Player

Juan Smith

Top Try Scorer

J van der Westhuizen (89)

Current Most Capped Player

John Smit/Victor Matfield

Best Rugby World Cup Result

Winner in 1995 and 2007

Head Coach

Peter de Villiers

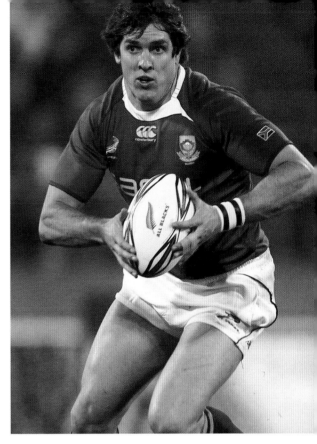

Clockwise from top: Jaque Fourie is a talented centre amongst a back division that attacks from any part of the field; Morne Steyn passes the ball against the Wallabies, 24 July, 2010; Prop Tendai Mtawarira prepares himself to scrummage against Wales in the 2010 Autumn International.

the number of caps and his partnership in the second row with Bakkies Botha is considered the most powerful in world rugby. Add to this the combination of the front rowers, CJ van der Linde and Bismarck du Plessis together with back row players, Juan Smith and Pierre Spies, then you have a very powerful pack, whilst in the backs Jean de Villiers, Morne Steyn, Bryan Habana and Ruan Pienaar will cause problems for any defence.

Their coach, Peter de Villiers, has been involved in more than one controversial incident since taking over from Jake White. Defending Schalk Burger for an alleged eye-gouging in the

second Test match against the Lions in 2009, de Villiers was quoted as saying, "If you are going to complain about every incident, we might as well go to the ballet shop and all get tutus". He then went on to antagonise the press when commenting, "We talk about murderers and gangsters. Our gangsters are the newspaper reporters. They spread lies and murder people without knowing it."

South Africa is in the weakest pool and should go through to at least the quarter-finals as pool winners with, realistically, only Wales seeming to bar their way. No one can take South Africa lightly when they get to the knock-out stages. They have such a tough mental edge and will only give up the title of World Champions to a very good side.

Previous spread, clockwise from top left: Schalk Berger is a fiery back row who caused controversy with foul play in the second Test against the Lions in 2009. Victor Matfield and Bakkies Botha are the best second row pairing in world rugby. Bryan Habana is back to his best as a try scoring wing.

Above: Gio Aplon scores for South Africa against Ireland in the match in Dublin in November 2010.
Right: Morne Steyn is a fly half that can kick prodigious goals from any part of the field, as he showed against the Lions in 2009.

Above: Victor Matfield and coach Peter de Villiers in discussion at a team run before the International against Ireland in November 2010.

Right: Willem Alberts scoring against Wales in November 2010 at Cardiff.

WALES

POOL D

Wales's record in the World Cup is most disappointing. Apart from a third place in the inaugural 1987 tournament when they beat Australia in the third place play-off match, they have, in the main, had a horrid time.

In 1991, they lost to Western Samoa and failed to reach the quarter-finals. Similarly, in 1995 they lost to Ireland and New Zealand in the pool games. They topped their pool in 1999, but then lost 24-7 to Australia.

England beat them in the quarter-finals in 2003 in Australia and they then had the ignominy of losing to Fiji in 2007. Apart from 1987, they have only made two quarter-finals and lost pool games to Tier 2 Pacific Island sides, Samoa and Fiji.

This is not good enough for such a proud country with a wonderful rugby history and the pressure will be on Warren Gatland to improve on this record.

Post amateurism, the Welsh club system has been subject to changes, which basically means that the country relies on four Regional sides to provide the bulk of their International players. Many of the old club names have disappeared from the top end of Welsh rugby and now operate in their own league below the Regional sides.

The four Regional sides, Ospreys, Scarlets, Cardiff Blues and Newport Dragons were formed by the then Welsh Rugby Union Chief Executive, David Moffett.

There have been simmering arguments under the surface between the Union and the Regions. In 2009 the argument ended up in the High Court in relation to player release. It was a nasty dirt-throwing argument which the governing body won.

In October 2010, an argument resurfaced between the WRU and Premier Rugby in England over the release of the Welsh players turning out

Below: James Hook can play in at least three positions behind the scrum, but always looks more dangerous at outside half. However, Wales has not been able to decide whether Hook or Stephen Jones is the best choice.

Fact File

Captain

Matthew Rees

Star Player

Shane Williams

Top Try Scorer

Shane Williams

Current Most Capped Player

Stephen Jones

Best Rugby World Cup Result

3rd in 1987

Head Coach

Warren Gatland

Right: Mike Phillips was the best scrum half in the world during the Lions tour of South Africa in 2009. He has the chance to regain that status in the World Cup.
Below right: Matthew Rees is the captain of Wales and knows the expectations of a nation.
Below: Stephen Jones will bring vast experience to the Welsh side.

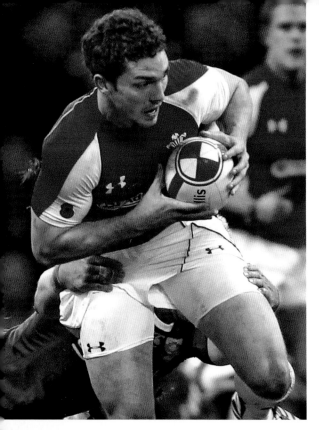

for English clubs in the Premiership. This disagreement still rumbles on with players finding it hard to satisfy two masters.

Wales, in fact, has the players to compete against any country, but has not shown that they can win key games. They won the Six Nations in 2008 but came fourth in 2009 and fourth in 2010. They lost their opening game in the Six Nations against England in Cardiff and their last game to France in Paris. In between they won their other three games but need to step up a considerable amount to put in a serious challenge for a place in the semi-finals of the World Cup.

They would expect to be in the top two of Pool D, but having lost to both Fiji and Samoa in previous World Cups, they will go into their games knowing that any lack of concentration will put them on an early plane home, particularly as they only managed to draw with Fiji in the Internationals played last autumn. They need a considerable amount of 'hwyl' that epitomised old Welsh sides of the 1970's.

In Mike Phillips they have a world-class scrum half, one of the best front rows in international rugby with Gethin Jenkins, Matthew Rees and Adam Jones, good wings with the maestro Shane Williams, plus Morgan Stoddart and newcomer George North, and a back rower to compete with Richie McCaw, Sam Warburton. What they have now got to do is see that the sum of the parts is more than enough to bring them victories, which has not always been achieved in the recent past.

Opposite top left: George North will cause problems on the wing because of his size and power.

Opposite top right: Alun Wyn-Jones is key to Wales winning the ball in the line-out with his mobility around the field. He will help Wales play an expansive game which will suit their three-quarters.

Opposite bottom: Sam Warburton could become one of the stars of the tournament.

Right: Shane Williams is back to his best after various injuries and wants to go out in his last World Cup on a high.

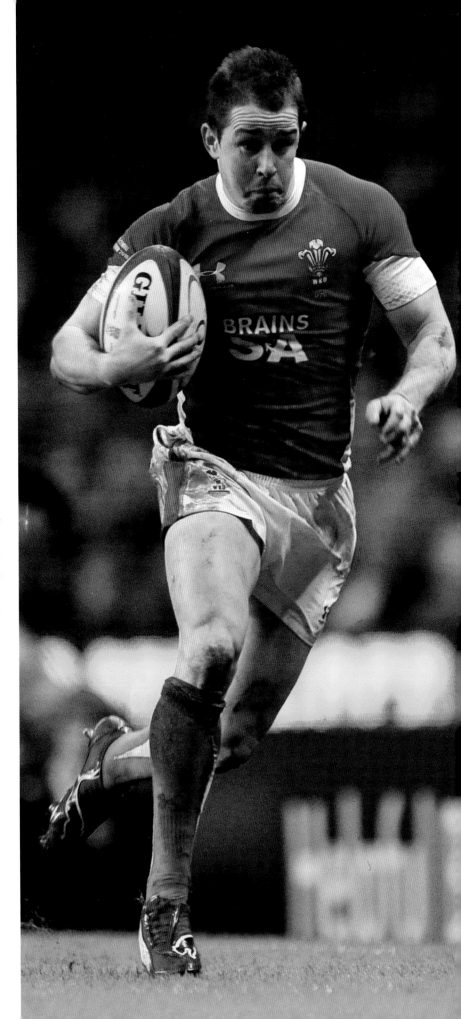

FIJI

POOL D

Rugby is considered to be the national sport of the country. Fiji has become famous for their success in Sevens and some blame the Fijians' obsession with this to be to the detriment of the fifteen-a-side game.

They competed in the first World Cup in 1987 and won through to the quarter-finals where they lost 31-16 to France. They lost all their games in the 1991 finals and did not qualify in 1995. 1999 saw them lose to England by 45-24 in the quarter-final play-offs and win only two games in the 2003 tournament.

In 2007 Fiji played exceptionally well to win three of their four pool games beating Japan, Canada, and an historic win over Wales, only losing to Australia. They played South Africa in the quarter-finals and went down 37-20, but making South Africa fight all the way.

They have been denied entry into the Super 14 Tournament in the Southern Hemisphere which has hindered the development of their domestic game and they only have teams from the Northern Hemisphere visiting on an irregular basis.

Professionalism has been a mixed blessing for the Fijian game. It has allowed them to develop some outstanding talent, but it has seen many of their most successful players move to other countries in both the Northern and Southern Hemispheres, which has devalued their own domestic competition.

Fiji does play in the IRB Pacific Rugby Cup, which was started in 2006 and involves Fiji, Samoa and Tonga. Fiji has two sides in the tournament that the Fiji Warriors won in 2009. There is also the ANZ Pacific Nations Cup in which Fiji play the Junior All Blacks, Samoa, Tonga and Japan. This has become a very successful tournament with a fervent following from the public.

The real problem for Fiji is the perennial club v country dispute with many of the leading professional players unavailable for the Pacific Nations Cup.

This situation will continue to occur until the Fijian Rugby Union finds another strong manager like Pio Bosco Tikoisuva who did an excellent job in 2007. They have the players. A look at their

Below: The Fiji side perform their pre-match ritual before facing Australia in the World Cup match in Montpellier in November 2007. If they perform as well as their Sevens side, they would be a match for any side. They are hoping the weather is kind to them in New Zealand and their backs have the firm ground that brings out the best in their play.

players overseas shows that the talent is there: Talemaitoga Tuapati, Gabiriele Lovobalavu, Netani Talei, Akapusi Qera, Seru Rabeni and the wonderful Sireli Bobo and Rupeni Caucaunibuca, if they can get them to play.

Get this group together with home-based players and nobody will go into a game with Fiji overconfident of success. As a Canadian coach once said on preparing to play against Fiji's expansive attacking style, "You blindfold yourself and spin around for ten times and then open your eyes and try and chase them down".

They have to aim to win three of their games against South Africa, Wales, Samoa and Namibia. Not an impossible task, but they need all their overseas players to be available.

Fact File

Captain

Deacon Manu

Star Player

Akapusi Qera

Top Try Scorer

Sainivalati Laulau (18)

Current Most Capped Player

Norman Ligairi

Best Rugby World Cup Result

Quarter Finals 1987 and 2007

Head Coach

Sam Domoni

Top: Seru Rabeni beats Tom Shanklin of Wales in the World Cup game in 2007.
Middle: Netani Talei on the charge in a Pacific Nations Cup match between Japan and Fiji in Tokyo, Japan in June 2008.
Bottom: Scrum half Nemia Kenatale passes the ball from the scrum during the Autumn International against Wales in Cardiff, November 2010 when Fiji held Wales to a draw. Wales are in the same pool as Fiji who will fancy their chances playing in front of a vociferous pro-Fiji crowd.

SAMOA

POOL D

Samoa has had some exceptional players over the last 20 years who were born there but did not play for their country of birth. All Blacks John Schuster and Va'aiga Tuigamala were both born in Samoa, but played for New Zealand.

Over the years they have lost numerous players to New Zealand, but have still been able to field very competitive sides and have appeared in every World Cup except 1987 when appearance was by invitation only.

Samoa's greatest World Cup triumph was in 1991 when they beat Wales at a stunned Cardiff Arms Park by 16-13.

Under their famous All Black coach, Michael Jones, Samoa was grouped in the 2007 World Cup with England, South Africa, Tonga and USA. They certainly did not do themselves justice, only having one win against the USA, and finished fourth in their pool. They had to go through qualifying to make the finals for 2011, but did this easily.

The rugby relationship that exists between New Zealand and Samoa is a very complex and contentious one. There is undoubtedly very close ties between the two countries which started with the mass Polynesian migration to New Zealand in the latter half of the twentieth century. Many players eligible for Samoa chose to play for the All Blacks, obviously recognising the financial and sporting rewards. Unfortunately, having committed themselves to the All Blacks, they became unavailable to ever play for Samoa.

In the 2007 World Cup there were 14 New Zealand-born players in the Samoan squad and five Samoan players in the New Zealand squad. Of the current players, a great number of the squad is playing in Europe or New Zealand.

For a nation that only started taking rugby seriously in the 1980's, Samoa has done remarkably well in the past 25 years. The country has a population of only 183,000 and comprises two large and four small islands, located 800 miles north-east of Fiji and 1800 miles north of New Zealand. But after the relative failure in the 2007 World Cup, the Samoan RFU decided, after

Below: The Samoan players perform their own pre-match ritual in Aberdeen, Scotland in November 2010. Samoa are in the same pool as Fiji and Namibia so they will aim for a second-place spot to progress to the quarter-finals.

an extensive review, to increase its National Selection Panel to include a member from New Zealand (Peter Fatialofa) and Australia (Tavita Sio) in an effort to keep up with the level of rugby played in Tier 1 countries. The success of the country's High Performance Unit has meant that, whereas the 1999 World Cup Squad comprised 29 overseas-based players in a squad of 30, the balance has swung much more towards home-based players where it is hoped 40% of them will be playing regularly in Samoa.

Four of their best players are playing at London Irish. Number 8, George Stowers, and backs, Sailosi Tagicakibau, Seilala Mapusua and Elvis Seveali'i. Wasps' David Lemi is one of the best wings playing in the Premiership and Alesana Tuilagi of Leicester gets a handful of tries against good defences. They also have an underrated full back, Paul Williams, and an improving scrum half, Kahn Fotuali'i. A good nucleus of top-class players that could cause shocks, particularly as they will spend time together before the start of the World Cup, which has not been the case for them in the years since 2007.

Fact File

Captain

Mahonri Schwalger

Star Player

Alesana Tuilagi

Top Try Scorer

Brian Lima (31)

Current Most Capped Player

Mahonri Schwalger

Best Rugby World Cup Result

Quarter Finals 1991 and 1995

Head Coach

Fuimaono Tafua

Top: Winger Lome Fa'atau hands off to South African wing, Bryan Habana, during the World Cup game at the Parc des Princes, Paris in September 2007.

Above: Alesana Tuilagi is tackled by Hale T Pole of Tonga in the World Cup of 2007.

NAMIBIA

Rugby is a popular team sport that was really introduced by migrants from South Africa from about 1960 onwards. The British and Irish Lions played in South West Africa – as the country was known before independence in 1990 – on a number of occasions from 1962.

Namibia came to international attention in 1991 when they beat an improving Italian side, and then defeated the touring Irish national side in two Tests by 15-6 and 26-15. They have been the consistent representative of Africa beyond South Africa itself, since 1999.

For a vast, sparsely populated country, with little infrastructure, players often have long distances to travel. The sport is popular among school children, but the Rugby Union-playing population in Namibia is still very small with only 19 clubs and around 7,500 registered players.

The Namibian national team are commonly known as the Welwitschia or Biltongboere. As well as competing in the last three World Cups, Namibia annually competes in the Africa Cup.

Since the 1999 World Cup, Namibia have struggled in the 2003 and 2007 competitions, suffering a record defeat of 142-0 against Australia in the 2003 tournament. They laboured in the qualifiers in 2007, suffering defeats to Kenya and Tunisia. However, they bounced back and after defeating Tunisia at home, they decisively beat Morocco in a two-legged eliminator and qualified.

The lowest-ranked team at the start of the 2007 World Cup, Namibia frustrated Ireland, scoring two tries and only lost by 17-32. However, they were well beaten against France, Argentina and Georgia, meaning they have been without a win in any game they have played in three World Cups.

In the qualifying stages for the 2011 World Cup they started in a very unconvincing style, just managing to win 13-10 against Senegal after a late try by Captain Jacques Nieuwenhuis. They finally won through to take their place in New Zealand by beating Tunisia 18-13 in Tunis and winning the second leg 22-10 in Windhoek. They have a very effective back row in Nieuwenhuis, Tinus du Plessis and Jacques Burger, big locks with Wacca Kazombiaze and Nico Esterhuizen plus new talent in Andre de Klerk and Jacky Bock.

Below: Nico Esterhuizen wins the ball in the line-out from Simon Easterby of Ireland.

Fact File

Captain
Kees Lensing

Star Player
Jacques Burger

Top Try Scorer
Gerhard Mans (27)

Current Most Capped Player
Kees Lensing/Jacques Burger

Best Rugby World Cup Result
Bottom of Pool 1999, 2003 and 2007

Head Coach
John Williams/Johan Diergaardt

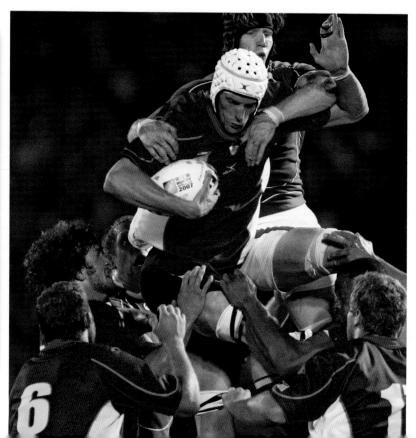

Namibia qualified for the 2011 World Cup under their head coach John Williams, formerly of South Africa, who coached at various levels in his home country. At the time of his appointment, Williams said, "My aim is to put pride back into Namibian rugby and to start winning some trophies. My ultimate aim will be to finish amongst the top eight teams at the 2011 World Cup".

With Wales and South Africa the favourites to go through in Pool D, it will be a massive effort for Namibia to advance past the pool stages or even to win a game.

It has been a magnificent effort for Namibia to again reach the finals, especially for a country with only 19 clubs and 7,500 registered players. Their head coach, John Williams, an ex-Springbok international, seeks continuing improvement in their results and this World Cup should show how far they have progressed.

Clockwise from top right: The Namibian side in a huddle before a World Cup game with the last words from Captain Kees Lensing; Lensing leads his team out onto the field before a training session in preparation for a game against France in the 2007 World Cup; Flanker Jacques Nieuwenhuis dives to score a try during a match against Ireland in 2007 World Cup played in Bordeaux; Jacques Nieuwenhuis wins the ball in a line-out.

STATISTICS

A South African Airways
jumbo jet with the slogan
'Good Luck Bookie' flies
over the stadium before the
1995 Rugby World Cup
Final between South Africa
and New Zealand at Ellis
Park, Johannesburg on
24 June, 1995.

PREVIOUS WINNERS OF THE WORLD CUP

Rugby World Cup 1987 (NZ & Australia)
Winner: NZ, Runner Up: France
Losing semi-finalists: Wales and Australia
PoT: Michael Jones NZ

Not many people were even conscious of the first World Cup which was supposed to be a one-off. The All Blacks were joint favourites with joint hosts Australia, but the Wallabies hype was short-lived as they succumbed to France in the semi-finals and then lost to Wales in the play-off for third place. David Kirk lifted the first William Webb Ellis Cup, as the winning All Black captain.

Rugby World Cup 1991 (England+)
Winner: Australia, Runner Up: England
Losing semi-finalists: Scotland & NZ
PoT: David Campese Australia

Once again, New Zealand arrived as firm favourites and beat England easily at Twickenham in the opening rounds, but lost their way against Australia in a semi-final. England clawed their way to the final and then changed their tactics from a forward-dominating game to a free-flowing game, which stunned everyone but ultimately played into the hands of the Wallabies, who kept their nerve to win 12-6.

Rugby World Cup 1995 (South Africa)
Winner: South Africa, Runner Up: NZ
Losing semi-finalists: France & England
PoT: Jonah Lomu NZ

Nelson Mandela turned up to the final wearing the No 6 shirt of Springbok Captain, Francois Pienaar. He received a standing ovation from a largely Afrikaans audience...the All Blacks complained afterwards that their food had been tampered with the night before and there was plenty of evidence of that in the dressing room and on the pitch. Nonetheless, the Springboks subdued Jonah Lomu and won the game in extra time with a drop goal from Joel Stransky.

Rugby World Cup 1999 (Wales+)
Winner: Australia, Runner Up: France
Losing semi-finalists: South Africa & NZ
PoT: Tim Horan Australia
France caused the upset of the tournament by beating the favourites New Zealand in a semi-final at Twickenham, having been almost out for the count at half time. The final was disappointing, unless you were a Wallaby supporter.

Rugby World Cup 2003 (Australia)
Winner: England, Runner Up: Australia
Losing semi-finalists: NZ and France
PoT: Jonny Wilkinson England
England was the clear favourite going into the event, which was unusual given this final was Down Under. Australia looked the only side that would really push them and so it proved as the final went into extra time until that drop goal by Jonny Wilkinson sealed an outstanding tournament.

Rugby World Cup 2007 (France+)
Winner: South Africa, Runner Up: England
Losing semi-finalists: France and Argentina
PoT: Juan Martin Hernandez Argentina
There were three real surprises – Argentina's opening win against France and then her progression to the semi-finals; France's wonderful victory in the quarter-final against New Zealand who at one time were coasting to a win; and England. England were thrashed in their opening fixture 36-0 by South Africa, but their forwards came of age and dominated the games against Australia in the quarter-final and France in the semis to qualify for a second consecutive final.

Rugby World Cup Standings
1987-2007

5 points for winning, 3 for Runner Up,
1 each for Semi-final

Australia: 14

England: 13

South Africa: 11

New Zealand: 11

France: 8

Wales: 1

Scotland: 1

Argentina: 1

World Cup Match Winning Kickers

1987 Grant Fox 17 for New Zealand
v France 29-9

1991 Michael Lynagh 8 for Australia
v England 12-6

1995 Joel Stransky 15 for SA
v New Zealand 15-12

1999 Matt Burke 25 for Australia
v France 35-12

2003 Jonny Wilkinson 15 for England
v Australia 20-17

2007 Percy Montgomery 12 for SA
v England 15-6

A team without a kicker
with a 75% success rate or
more is in serious trouble.

Below: Jonny Wilkinson kicking the drop goal that won the 2003 World Cup for England against Australia in extra time after the two sides finished 17 points each in normal time.

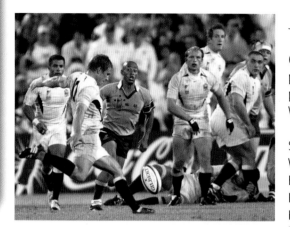

Above: Felipe Contepomi of Argentina showing the classic way to hold the ball in two hands in a match between France and Argentina in Montpellier, November 2010.

Trivia

Two match-ups occurring twice in the same World Cup happened in 2007. Argentina defeated France in the opening match 17-12, and went on to beat them 34-10 in the third place play-off. South Africa beat England 36-0 in the group stages, and went on to play them in the final, winning 15-6.

Jonny Wilkinson, with 15 points in 2003 and 6 in 2007, is the only player to have scored points in two Rugby World Cup finals.

Six players have won the World Cup twice: John Eales, Dan Crowley, Phil Kearns, Jason Little, Tim Horan (all for Australia in 1991 and 1999) and Os du Randt (for South Africa in 1995 and 2007). All won once in the amateur era and once in the professional era (the 1995 World Cup was the final major event of the amateur era).

England are the only nation to have reached two Rugby World Cup finals; 1991 and 2007, having previously lost games in the opening stages of the tournament.

The team involved in the most World Cup opening matches is Argentina, who participated in the first three World Cup openers of the professional era — losing to Wales and Australia in 1999 and 2003 respectively, and defeating France in 2007. New Zealand will equal this mark when it opens the 2011 World Cup against Tonga; the All Blacks defeated Italy in 1987 and England in 1991.

Winning Coaches
Brian Lochore New Zealand (1987)
Bob Dwyer Australia (1991)
Kitch Christie South Africa (1995)
Rod MacQueen Australia (1999)
Clive Woodward England (2003)
Jake White South Africa (2007)

Winning Captains
David Kirk New Zealand (1987)
Nick Farr-Jones Australia (1991)
Francois Pienaar South Africa (1995)
John Eales Australia (1999)
Martin Johnson England (2003)
John Smit South Africa (2007)

Far Left: Clive Woodward holds up the Webb Ellis World Cup Trophy after England's defeat of Australia in the final at the Telstra Stadium, Sydney in 2003. This was England's first win in the Cup, made even more special having been achieved on Australian soil.
Left: John Eales, the Captain of Australia, and team mate George Gregan hold the Webb Ellis Trophy after winning the final of the 1999 Rugby World Cup against France, played at the Millennium Stadium in Cardiff, Wales.

Year	Attendance	TV audience	Gross Commercial income	Net Surplus
1987	600,000	300 million	£3.3 million	£1.0 million
1991	1 million	1.75 billion	£23.6 million	£4.1 million
1995	1 million	2.67 billion	£30.3 million	£17.6 million
1999	1.75 million	3.1 billion	£70 million	£47.3 million
2003	1.8 million	3.4 billion	£81.8 million	£64.3 million
2007	2.2 million	4.2 billion		£122.4 million

Above: A section of the crowd at the 2007 match between Australia and Japan in Lyons, France. The fans are doing the Mexican wave.

Right: Wayne Barnes, the English referee, officiating in the 2007 World Cup in a game between Ireland and Georgia in Bordeaux.

Tickets Sales

Ticket sales for the Rugby World Cup were broken up into three phases. The first phase was released in November 2005, when members of the European rugby community, such as officials, players and so on were given the opportunity for various packages. Upon the release of the second-phase ticketing scheme, more than 100,000 tickets were sold in the first ten hours of release. The remaining tickets — individual tickets and tickets to the semi-finals — were released in phase three in November 2006. In June 2007, it was announced that 2 million of the 2.4 million tickets had been sold in advance of the tournament.

Sponsors

Worldwide partners for the tournament were Société Générale, GMF, Électricité de France, Peugeot, Visa and SNCF, and official sponsors included Heineken, Vediorbis, Capgemini, Orange, Toshiba and Emirates. Gilbert provided the tournament balls – the Gilbert Synergie match ball was used throughout the tournament. This continued Gilbert's involvement with the World Cup, the company having provided the Barbarian (1995), Revolution (1999) and Xact (2003) balls in the past. Along with Gilbert, the official suppliers were Adidas, Coca-Cola, Clifford Chance, Goodyear and McDonalds. Official Broadcaster was TF1.

Squads

Each country was allowed a squad of 30 players for the tournament. These squads had to be submitted to the International Rugby Board by a deadline of 14 August 2007. Once the squad was submitted a player could be replaced if injured, but would not be allowed to return to the squad.

Match Officials

The 2007 Rugby World Cup officials were appointed in late April 2007, with 12 referees and 13 touch judges being chosen to officiate during the pool stage. In the knock-out stage the 12 referees also acted as touch judges, with referee appointments being based on performance in previous matches and selected for neutrality.

Referees came from seven different nationalities and three of them made their Rugby World Cup debut. The touch judges came from 10 different countries. Tony Spreadbury of England officiated in the opening game between France and Argentina at the Stade de France and Irishman Alain Rolland refereed the final.

Rugby World Cup 2007 Statistics

City	Country	Stadium	Capacity
Paris	France	Stade de France	80,000
Cardiff	Wales	Millennium Stadium	73,350
Edinburgh	Scotland	Murrayfield	68,000
Marseille	France	Stade Vélodrome	59,500
Paris	France	Parc de Princes	47,870
Lens	France	Stade Félix-Bollaert	41,400
Lyons	France	Stade de Gerland	41,100
Nante	France	Stade de la Beaujoire	38,100
Toulouse	France	Stadium de Toulouse	35,700
Saint-Étienne	France	Geoffrey Guichard	35,650
Bordeaux	France	Chaban-Delmas	34,440
Montpellier	France	Stade de la Mosson	33,900

Richie McCaw, the most capped New Zealand captain, leading out the All Black side to the quarter-final game between New Zealand and France. New Zealand has not won the Cup since the inaugural tournament in 1987.

2007 Tournament details

Host nation	France
Dates	7th September - 20th October
No. of nations	20 (91 qualifying)
Champions	South Africa
Runner-up	England
Matches played	48
Attendance	2,263,223 (47,150 per match)
Top Scorer	Percy Montgomery (105)
Most tries	Bryan Habana (8)

IRB World Rankings - 07 April 2011		
Position	**Member Union**	**Points**
1 (1)	New Zealand	93.19
2 (2)	Australia	87.45
3 (3)	South Africa	86.44
4 (4)	Ireland	82.51
5 (5)	England	82.48
6 (6)	France	82.06
7 (7)	Wales	79.55
8 (8)	Argentina	78.97
9 (9)	Scotland	77.35
10 (10)	Fiji	74.05
11 (11)	Samoa	74.02
12 (12)	Italy	73.54
13 (13)	Japan	71.45
14 (14)	Georgia	70.16
15 (15)	Canada	69.19
16 (16)	USA	67.69
17 (17)	Tonga	67.35
18 (18)	Romania	65.34
19 (19)	Russia	63.17
20 (20)	Portugal	61.81
21 (21)	Uruguay	60.94
22 (22)	Namibia	60.66
23 (23)	Spain	59.43
24 (24)	Chile	56.68
25 (25)	Morocco	56.11

For Australia, South Africa and New Zealand, the 2011 Tri Nations series will serve as the primary preparation for the tournament. In the Northern Hemisphere, a series of friendlies played in August 2011 replace the annual tours to the Southern Hemisphere.

Seeding

Seeding of teams for the 2011 World Cup was based on their respective IRB world rankings.

The top four at the 2007 Rugby World Cup (South Africa, England, Argentina, and France) were not therefore allocated top pool spots, but "the rankings are now very well established and provide us with a credible and succinct way of seeding teams for the Rugby World Cup pool draw", according to Rugby World Cup Ltd (RWCL) chairman Syd Millar.

The draw was conducted in December 2008 and used the world rankings as of 1 December 2008, after the Northern Hemisphere Autumn Internationals.

The teams were placed into three bands depending on their seedings at the time, with one team from each band in each of the groups.

The rankings and bands were therefore: New Zealand (1), South Africa (2), Australia (3) and Argentina (4); Wales (5), England (6), France (7) and Ireland (8); Scotland (9), Fiji (10), Italy (11) and Tonga (12). The full draw and venues for the tournament were announced on 12 March 2009.

The opening match will see the hosts, New Zealand, take on Tonga. This will be the first World Cup since 1995 in which the opening match does not involve Argentina.

Right: Martin Johnson performs the hongi with a Maori woman during the Rugby World Cup draw in London in 2008.

Venues

The 13 venues for the 2011 Rugby World Cup were confirmed on 12 March 2009.

A number of the venues announced are undergoing redevelopment to increase capacity for the event. Dunedin is currently building a new stadium named Forsyth Barr Stadium at University Plaza, due for completion in August 2011. If completed on schedule, it will be used instead of Carisbrook.

Left: The Westpac stadium in Wellington, where seven games will be held during the World Cup 2011.

2011 World Cup Stadia

City	Stadium	Capacity	No. of matches
Auckland	Eden Park	60,000	9
Wellington	Westpac Stadium	36,000	8
Rotorua	International Stadium	34,000	3
Dunedin	Forsyth Barr	30,500	5
Hamilton	Waikato Stadium	25,800	3
Auckland	North Harbour	25,000	4
Whangatei	Okara Park	25,000	2
New Plymouth	Yarrow Stadium	25,000	3
Napier	McLean Park	22,000	2
Nelson	Trafalgar Park	20,080	3
Plamerston North	Arena Manawatu	18,000	2
Invercargill	Rugby Park	17,000	3

Helpful Internet Sites

www.google.com/alerts
   - sign up for daily email updates
www.bbc.co.uk/rugby
www.bbc.co.uk/2011rugbyworldcup
www.itv.com/sport/rugby/rugbyworldcup
www.rugbyfootballhistory.com
www.planetrugby.com
www.trinationsrugby.net

www.rugbyweek.com
www.theglobalherald.com
www.espnscrum.com
www.therugbyblog.co.uk
www.worldcupweb.com
www.rugbynz2011.com
www.rugbyworldcup.com
www.irb.com

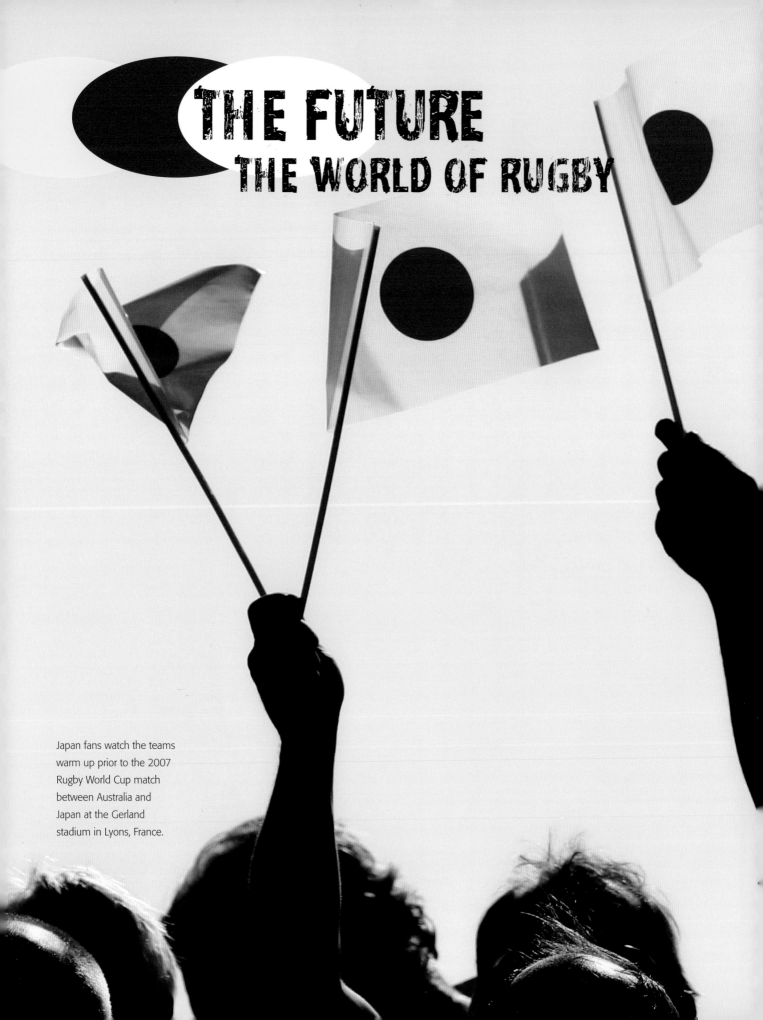

THE FUTURE
THE WORLD OF RUGBY

Japan fans watch the teams warm up prior to the 2007 Rugby World Cup match between Australia and Japan at the Gerland stadium in Lyons, France.

Future of the Rugby World Cup: 2015, 2019 and beyond

The IRB has been painfully slow in moving the game forward. It likes to pat itself on the back about the television coverage of the RWC, claiming it is now the third most-watched finals of any sport. This precludes sports such a Formula 1 and golf which have larger week-by-week followings when in season.

Following the debacle of the way the 2011 Rugby World Cup was awarded, there has been an outbreak of IRB sanity in determining the bids for the next two World Cups. For RWC 2011 the New Zealand tax payer has guaranteed a payment of $40m to the IRB (in other words, the actual Cup will make a loss for the host country which is unprecedented). Japan's unsuccessful bid for RWC 2011 would have made substantial money and it was underwritten by its leading global companies.

The lessons seemed to have been learned. At its meeting on 28 July, 2010 the IRB considered four bids for offers for RWC 2015 and RWC 2019 and it was England and Japan who succeeded in their bids, after having been perhaps unfairly sidelined in earlier bids.

The England bid is likely to be profitable for the host country and the IRB to the tune of £150m. Japan's plans include taking the game to Hong Kong and South Korea. By awarding the RWC 2011 to New Zealand, the IRB delayed the development of the game in China, a country which is still likely to have the most rugby players of any nation within the next five years. Political relationships between China and Japan have improved over the past decade and maybe the IRB could lean on the Japanese to allow some games in 2019 to be played in Shanghai.

The organisation of the IRB itself

There are two urgent reforms required immediately. The first is to do with the voting rights of the IRB's Council. At present, England, Wales, Scotland, Ireland, France, New Zealand, South Africa and Australia each have two votes (16 votes); Canada, Argentina, Italy and Japan each have one seat (4 votes), as do the regional associations in Europe, Asia, Africa and the Americas (4 votes). Accordingly, the Council is structured to ensure the game remains in the perception of its founders. These rules meant that Japan lost RWC 2011 by only one vote to New Zealand. Until there is one vote per country, progress to make rugby a truly global game will be painfully slow.

The second is to find a permanent voice for the players. The professional game makes rugby what it is. It is the driving force for change, yet the

Below: England's Martin Thomas and Japan's Noboru Mashimo celebrate after hearing the IRB decision to award the World Cup to England in 2015 and 2019 to Japan.

Right: An excited Chinese supporter cheering his side during the China versus Hong Kong semi-final in the 16th Asian Games, November 2010. Hong Kong won 19-14. Where will China be in terms of rugby in 2019?

professionals have no presence on the Council. We recommend eight professional players, past or current (most likely to be past), be appointed to the Council.

At some stage, as the women's game develops, the two organisations should consider merging.

Rugby in the Olympics: Rio de Janeiro, 2016

The International Olympic Committee is a large, unwieldy organisation which likes to think of itself as an independent state. Indeed, former President Juan Samaranch sought Observer status at the United Nations and also lobbied unsuccessfully to be awarded the Nobel Peace prize.

Rugby has not been in the Olympics since 1924 and the IRB and others had lobbied unsuccessfully for its re-introduction over the past thirty years. The breakthrough came at the IOC Session in Copenhagen in October 2009, when Rugby Sevens competed with golf for two available spaces in the 2016 Olympics.

The IRB used a number of high-profile people and events to influence the IOC. In March 2009, two senior delegates from the IOC attended the Rugby World Cup Sevens in Dubai at the invitation of the IRB. Jonah Lomu and Lawrence Dallaglio were announced as ambassadors for the bid at the same time and in April Waisale Serevi was made an ambassador to coincide with the Oceania National Olympic Committee's general assembly. In May the IRB announced that they

would drop the Rugby World Cup Sevens to make the Olympics the premier event in international Rugby Sevens.

It was a huge effort by the rugby community but it paid off on 9 October 2009 when the IOC finally voted to include Rugby Sevens in the 2016 games.

Separate competitions for men and women will be held, using a similar format to the existing IRB Sevens World Series. The IRB had originally proposed including 12 teams of each sex, but when two IOC members asked why only 12 teams were included, IRB Chief Executive Mike Miller responded, "We followed the guidance of the Executive Members of the IOC, but if the IOC feels we should have more teams, we will add more."

Above: Waisale Serevi of Fiji, one of the greats of the seven-a-side game, attempts to beat a Canadian opponent in the IRB Sevens World Series at Adelaide in April 2007.

Left: Lawrence Dallaglio and Jonah Lomu attending the Dubai Rugby World Cup Sevens in March 2009 and signing the "Reaching Out" wall for the Rugby Sevens Olympic campaign.

It has taken a decade, but rugby has made it back to the Olympics, perhaps cheered on by IOC President Jacques Rogge who is a former player for Belgium. It will be the seven-a-side version for both men and women at the 2016 Olympics in Rio de Janeiro. Sevens is the "beach-volleyball" version of the senior game, simpler to play, faster on the eye and a better television spectacle. Hopefully it will lead to a boom in the number of boys and girls wanting to play this version of the game. It's all good and perhaps by 2020, Sevens will seriously rival its 15-a-side cousin.

There is one issue which will not go away and that is the endemic corruption in sport in tier 2 and tier 3 countries which has bedevilled FIFA, the IAAF and the IOC. The IRB must ensure that the funding from the IOC is channelled through them first and not through each country's National Olympic Committee.

Zealand, Samoa and the United States and the winner will be announced shortly.

Prior to their triumph in 2010, New Zealand had won three times, in 1998 against USA, and in 2002 and 2006 against England. England won in 1994 against USA and USA won the first tournament in 1991, beating England.

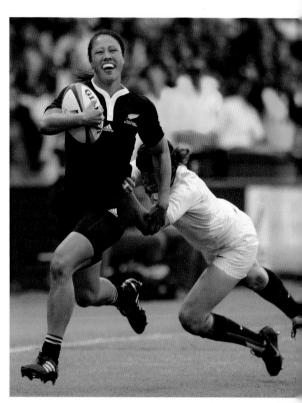

Women's Rugby World Cup 2014

After the stunningly successful Women's World Cup in England in 2010, won by the All Black Ferns, the hosts for 2014 will have their work cut out.

Over 30,000 supporters attended the 17-day tournament which culminated in New Zealand winning their fourth successive title, beating England 13-10 in front of a record 13,253 at the Twickenham Stoop stadium. The tournament was screened live to 127 countries.

Bids to stage the next Women's Rugby World Cup have been received from Kazakhstan, New

Rugby World Cup Sevens: Men's and Women's Russia, 2013

The inaugural tournament for the Melrose Cup, named after the Scottish border town, the birthplace of Rugby Sevens, was held in 1993 and won by England.

Wales are the current World Champions, having won the competition in 2009. Fiji has won the tournament twice. New Zealand and England have each won once.

The 2009 Rugby World Cup Sevens for Men and Women was held in Dubai during the first weekend of March 2009.

Wales, Samoa, Argentina and Kenya combined to stun the rugby world by defeating the traditional powerhouses New Zealand, England, South Africa and Fiji in the quarter-finals. Guaranteeing a new Melrose Cup winner, Wales and Argentina met in the final, with Wales triumphing 19-12. Wales' Taliesin Selley was named player of the tournament.

Below: New Zealand celebrate victory over England in the Women's World Cup final at the Twickenham Stoop, England.

Right: Carla Hohepa of New Zealand is tackled by Joanna McGilchrist of England during the Women's World Cup Final in September 2010.

The inaugural Women's Rugby World Cup Sevens tournament saw Australia edge out New Zealand 15-10 in extra-time to become the first winners of the Women's Rugby Sevens World Cup. Meanwhile, England defeated Canada 12-0 in the Bowl.

Women's Rugby Sevens was included in the IRB's successful bid to reintroduce rugby to the Olympics in 2016. It is also bidding for inclusion in the Commonwealth Games in 2018. The 2013 finals will be held in Russia.

Refereeing

If there is one issue that could determine the success or otherwise of the World Cup, the refereeing of the scrums is at the top of the list.

A whole chapter could be devoted to this subject alone and many scrummaging experts have put forward their answer to the problem of contact at the scrum, the number of collapsed scrums and the lottery of penalties awarded.

In some games nearly 10 minutes out of the 80 are taken up in the setting and resetting of collapsed front rows, with referees losing their patience and handing out penalties, seemingly, to some critics, on a random basis.

The problem with the crouch, touch, pause, engage order is the length of time between the pause and contact varying so much between referees that the players become more and more frustrated with a ton or so of prime beef waiting behind them, as they hold on precariously for the referee's last instruction in the sequence. The scrum goes down on impact, a penalty is awarded and a tight game is won or lost on such decisions.

Consistency in the timing of the exercise in setting scrums will be important, but more important will be the players' attitude to how they want to play the game. Let us hope that the sides do not use the scrums for slowing down the game and are given a chance to develop their game across the whole of the field by playing 15-a-side rugby.

The referees have enormous responsibility and the success of the World Cup will depend on their skill.

Left: Fans enjoy the Hong Kong Sevens that is part of the IRB World Sevens. There are eight various tournaments around the world, culminating in the side top of the points table being declared the Sevens champions for the year.

Below left: Tricia Brown of Australia scores a try during the Women's World Cup in 2010 against Wales, played at the Surrey Sports Park, Guildford.

Below: Alain Rolland of Ireland officiating during a RBS Six Nations Championship match between Wales and England in Cardiff, February 2011.

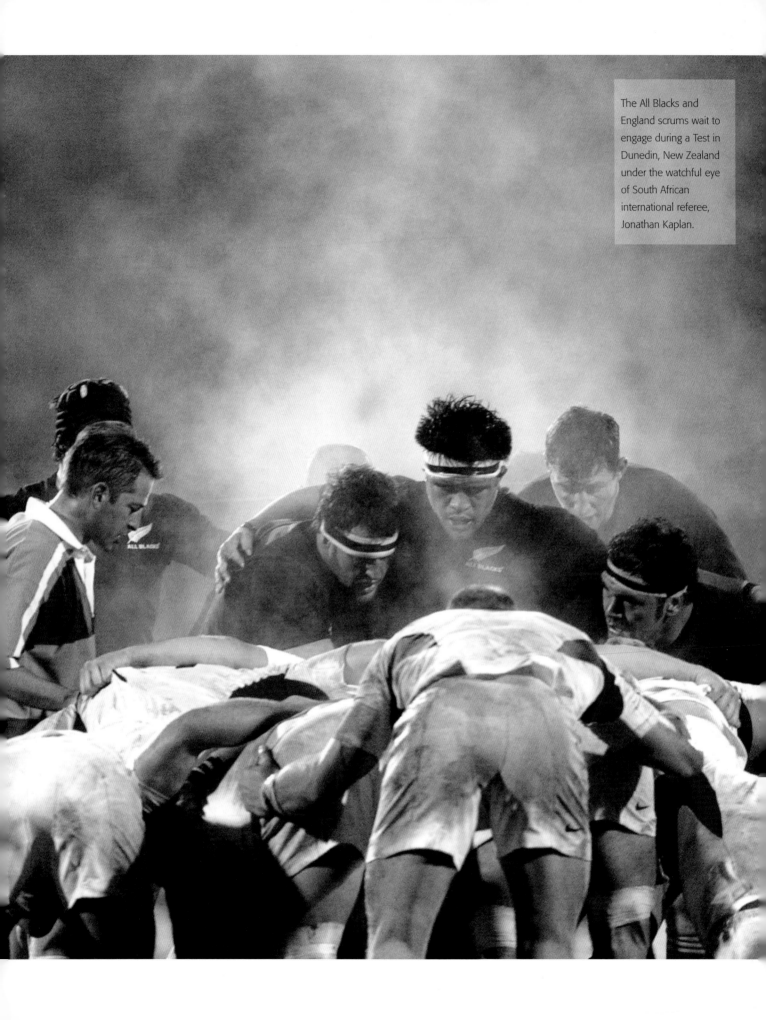

The All Blacks and England scrums wait to engage during a Test in Dunedin, New Zealand under the watchful eye of South African international referee, Jonathan Kaplan.